IRA GERSHWIN™
SONGBOOK

CONTENTS

INTRODUCTION

This is a very special book. The publication of any collection of songs by Ira Gershwin would be an occasion to Strike Up The Band, but this book goes far beyond the call of duty by including a large number of lyrical premieres.

For the first time, male versions of *The Girl I Love* and *Someone To Watch Over Me* are available. Additional lyrics are supplied for *Embraceable You*, *'S Wonderful* and *I Can't Get Started*. Other songs are printed in complete editions, personally approved by Ira Gershwin.

Many early songs (bringing collector's prices for original copies) are once again available.

It is the editors' sincere hope that this memorial collection of songs by one of America's greatest lyricists will create many happy hours of rhythm and rhyme.

MICHAEL FEINSTEIN, Editor

OH ME, OH MY!

He

Little girly,
Late and early,
You'll be on my mind—
For you're just the kind
I tried so long to find.
When you're near me,
When you cheer me,
I can plainly see,
Love is everything that
It's cracked up to be.

Refrain

Oh me! oh my! oh you-oo!
No other girl will do.
Cares would be forever ended,
And this world would be so splendid,
If you cared enough, dear, to be true.
Oh me! oh my! oh you-oo!
Those lips! Those eyes of blue!
You're so lovely, you're so sweet.
You simply lift me off my feet.
Oh me! oh my! oh you!

OH ME! OH MY!

Words by
ARTHUR FRANCIS*

Music by
VINCENT YOUMANS

Moderato con moto

Lit - tle girl - ie, late and earl - y, You'll be on my mind
For you're just the kind I tried so long to find;
When you're near me, when you cheer me I can plain - ly see Love is

*Pseudonym for Ira Gershwin early in his career.

OH ME, OH MY!

She

In replying
I am trying
To be shy and coy,
But, oh wonder boy,
I can't restrain my joy.
Something tells me
And compells me
To say you were right
In believing love may
Often come at sight.

Refrain

Oh me! oh my! oh You-oo!
What can a girly do!
I find you so fascinating
That my heart keeps palpitating
In a way that thrills me through and through.
Oh me! oh my! oh you-oo!
I'm sure I could be true.
You're so splendid—so ideal,
That I keep wond'ring if you're real.
Oh me! oh my! oh you!

I'LL BUILD A STAIRWAY TO PARADISE

All you preachers
Who delight in panning the dancing teachers,
Let me tell you there are a lot of features
Of the dance that carry you through
The Gates of Heaven.

It's madness
To be always sitting around in sadness,
When you could be learning the steps of Gladness.
(You'll be happy when you can do
Just six or seven.)

Begin today. You'll find it nice:
The quickest way to Paradise.
When you practice,
Here's the thing to know—
Simply say as you go:

Refrain (Con spirito)

I'll build a Stairway to Paradise,
   With a new Step ev'ry day.
I'm going to get there at any price;
   Stand aside, I'm on my way!

   I got the blues
   And up above it's so fair;
      Shoes,
   Go on and carry me there!
I'll build a Stairway to Paradise
   With a new Step ev'ry day.

I'll Build A Stairway To Paradise

Words by
B. G. DeSYLVA and IRA GERSHWIN

Music by
GEORGE GERSHWIN

OH, LADY BE GOOD!

1

Listen to my tale of woe,
It's terribly sad, but true:
    All dressed up, no place to go,
Each ev'ning I'm awf'ly blue.
        I must win some winsome miss;
        Can't go on like this.
    I could blossom out, I know,
With somebody just like you.
            So—

Refrain

Oh, sweet and lovely lady, be good.
    Oh, lady, be good to me!
I am so awf'ly misunderstood,
    So, lady, be good to me.
Oh, please have some pity—
I'm all alone in this big city.
        I tell you
I'm just a lonesome babe in the wood,
    So, lady, be good to me.

2

Auburn and brunette and blonde,
I love 'em all, tall or small.
    But somehow they don't grow fond,
They stagger but never fall.
        Winter's gone, and now it's Spring!
        Love! where is thy sting?
    If somebody won't respond,
I'm going to end it all,
            So——

Refrain

Oh, sweet and lovely lady, be good.
    Oh lady, be good to me.
I am so awf'ly misunderstood,
    So, lady, be good to me.
This is tulip weather—
So let's put two and two together
        I tell you
I'm just a lonesome babe in the wood,
    So, lady, be good to me.

OH, LADY BE GOOD!

Music and Lyrics by
GEORGE GERSHWIN and IRA GERSHWIN

THE MAN I LOVE

When the mellow moon begins to beam,
Ev'ry night I dream a little dream;
And of course Prince Charming is the theme:
      The he
      For me.
Although I realize as well as you
It is seldom that a dream comes true,
      To me it's clear
      That he'll appear.

Refrain

Some day he'll come along,
  The man I love;
And he'll be big and strong,
  The man I love;
And when he comes my way,
I'll do my best to make him stay.

He'll look at me and smile—
  I'll understand;
And in a little while
  He'll take my hand;
And though it seems absurd,
I know we both won't say a word.

Maybe I shall meet him Sunday,
  Maybe Monday—maybe not;
Still I'm sure to meet him one day—
  Maybe Tuesday
  Will be my good news day.

He'll build a little home
  Just meant for two;
From which I'll never roam—
  Who would? Would you?
And so all else above,
I'm waiting for the man I love.

THE GIRL I LOVE

He

Some day she'll come along,
  The girl I love;
Her smile will be a song,
  The girl I love;
And when she comes my way,
I'll do my best to make her stay.

I'll look at her and smile—
  She'll understand;
And in a little while
  I'll take her hand;
And though it seems absurd,
  I know we both won't say a word.

May I shall meet her Sunday,
  Maybe Monday—maybe not;
Still I'm sure to meet her one day—
  Maybe Tuesday
  Will be my good news day.

For her I'll do and dare
  As ne'er before;
Our hopes and fears we'll share—
  For evermore;
And so all else above,
I'm waiting for the girl I love.

THE MAN I LOVE

Music and Lyrics by
GEORGE GERSHWIN and IRA GERSHWIN

When the mel-low moon be-gins to beam, Ev-'ry night I dream a lit-tle dream,

And of course Prince Charm-ing is the theme, The he for me. Al-

FASCINATING RHYTHM

Got a little rhythm, a rhythm, a rhythm
  That pit-a-pats through my brain;
    So darn persistent,
    The day isn't distant
When it'll drive me insane.
  Comes in the morning
  Without any warning,
And hangs around me all day.
  I'll have to sneak up to it
  Someday, and speak up to it.
I hope it listens when I say:

  Refrain

  Fascinating Rhythm,
You've got me on the go!
  Fascinating Rhythm,
    I'm all a-quiver.

  What a mess you're making!
The neighbors want to know
  Why I'm always shaking
    Just like a flivver.

Each morning I get up with the sun—
    Start a-hopping,
    Never stopping—
To find at night no work has been done.

    I know that
    Once it didn't matter—
  But now you're doing wrong;
    When you start to patter
      I'm so unhappy.

    Won't you take a day off?
  Decide to run along
    Somewhere far away off—
      And make it snappy!

Oh, how I long to be the man I used to be!
  Fascinating Rhythm,
Oh, won't you stop picking on me?

FASCINATING RHYTHM

Music and Lyrics by
GEORGE GERSHWIN and IRA GERSHWIN

Got a lit-tle rhy-thm, A rhy-thm, a rhy-thm That pit-a-pats through my brain. So darn per-sis-tent, The day is-n't dis-tant When it-'ll drive me in-sane. Comes in the morn-ing With-

THAT CERTAIN FEELING

He

Knew it from the start—
Love would play a part—
Felt that feeling
        Come a stealing,
In my lonesome heart.

She

It would be ideal—
If that's the way you feel,
But tell me
        Is it really real?

He
        You gave me . . .
    Refrain
That certain feeling—
The first time I met you.
  I hit the ceiling
I could not forget you,
    You were completely sweet;
    Oh, what could I do?
        I wanted phrases
        To sing your praises.

That certain feeling—
The one that they all love—
    No use concealing
I've got what they call love.
        Now we're together
        Let's find out whether
You're feeling that feeling too.

She

I have symptoms, too,
Just the same as you.
When they centered,
    When they entered
In my heart, I knew.

Brighter is the day—
Since you've come my way;
Believe it
    When you hear me say:
    You gave me . . .

Refrain

That certain feeling—
The first time I met you.
    That certain feeling
I could not forget you.
    I felt it happen
    Just as you came in view.
        Grew sort of dizzy;
        Thought, "Gee, who is he?"

That certain feeling—
I'm here to confess, it
    Is so appealing
No words can express it.
        I cannot hide it,
        I must confide it:
I'm feeling that feeling too.

THAT CERTAIN FEELING

Music and Lyrics by
GEORGE GERSHWIN and IRA GERSHWIN

REFRAIN

HOW LONG HAS THIS BEEN GOING ON?

He

As a tot, when I trotted in little velvet
          panties,
I was kissed by my sisters, my cousins and
          my aunties.
Sad to tell, it was Hell—an Inferno worse
          than Dante's.

     So, my dear, I swore,
     "Never, nevermore!"
On my list I insisted that kissing must be
          crossed out.
Now I find I was blind, and, oh lady, how
          I've lost out!

Refrain

I could cry salty tears;
Where have I been all these years?
     Little wow,
     Tell me now:
How long has this been going on?

There were chills up my spine,
And some thrills I can't define.
     Listen, sweet,
     I repeat:
How long has this been going on?

Oh, I feel that I could melt;
     Into heaven I'm hurled—
I know how Columbus felt
     Finding another world.

Kiss me once, then once more.
What a dunce I was before!
     What a break—
     For heaven's sake!
How long has this been going on?

She

'Neath the stars at bazaars often I've had to
          caress men.
Five or ten dollars I'd collect from all
          those yes-men.
Don't be sad, I must add that they meant no more
          than chessmen.

     Darling, can't you see
     'Twas for charity?
Though these lips have made slips, it was never
          really serious.
Who'd 'a' thought I'd be brought to a state
          that's so delirious?

Refrain

I could cry salty tears;
Where have I been all these years?
     Listen, you—
     Tell me, do:
How long has this been going on?

What a kick—how I buzz!
Boy, you click as no one does!
     Hear me, sweet,
     I repeat:
How long has this been going on?

Dear, when in your arms I creep—
     That divine rendezvous—
Don't wake me, if I'm asleep,
     Let me dream that it's true.

Kiss me twice, then once more—
That makes thrice, let's make it four!
     What a break—
     For heaven's sake!
How long has this been going on?

HOW LONG HAS THIS BEEN GOING ON?

Music and Lyrics by
GEORGE GERSHWIN and IRA GERSHWIN

SUNNY DISPOSISH

Any time the thunder starts to rumble down,
  Don't let hope tumble down,
  Or castles crumble down.
If the blues appear, just make the best of them,
  Just make a jest of them,
  Don't be possessed of them.
At the risk of sounding rather platitudinous—
Here's what I believe should be the attitude in us:

Refrain

  A sunny disposish,
  Will always see you through—
When up above the skies are blah,
  'Stead of being blue.
Mister trouble makes our faces grow long,
But a smile will have him saying "so long!"

  It really doesn't pay,
  To be a gloomy pill—
It's absolutely most redic'
  Positively sil'.
The rain may pitter patter,
It really doesn't matter,
  For life can be delish—
  With a sunny disposish.

Second Verse

Must confess I like your way of viewing it,
  No use in rueing it,
  When gloom is blueing it.
Taking your advice the sad and weary'll
  Have no material,
  To be funerial.
It's a thought that they should be swallowing, my dear,
Look at me, already you're a following my dear.

SUNNY DISPOSISH

Words by
IRA GERSHWIN

Music by
PHILIP CHARIG

42

SOMEONE TO WATCH OVER ME

There's a saying old
    Says that love is blind.
Still, we're often told
    "Seek and ye shall find."
So I'm going to seek a certain lad I've had in mind.
    Looking ev'rywhere,
        Haven't found him yet;
    He's the big affair
        I cannot forget—
Only man I ever think of with regret.
I'd like to add his initial to my monogram.
Tell me, where is the shepherd for this lost lamb?

Refrain

There's a somebody I'm longing to see:
    I hope that he
    Turns out to be
Someone who'll watch over me.

I'm a little lamb who's lost in the wood;
    I know I could
    Always be good
To one who'll watch over me.

    Although he may not be the man some
    Girls think of as handsome,
        To my heart he'll carry the key.

Won't you tell him, please, to put on some speed.
    Follow my lead?
    Oh, how I need
Someone to watch over me.

SOMEONE TO WATCH OVER ME

Music and Lyrics by
GEORGE GERSHWIN and IRA GERSHWIN

SOMEONE TO WATCH OVER ME
(MALE VERSION)

Refrain

There's a somebody I've wanted to see;
  I hope that she
  Turns out to be
Someone who'll watch over me.

I'm a little lamb who's lost in the wood;
  I know I could
  Always be good
To one who'll watch over me.

She may be far;
She may be nearby;
I'm promising hereby,
  To my heart she'll carry the key.

And this world would be like heaven if she'd
  Follow my lead
  Oh, how I need
Someone to watch over me.

CLAP YO' HANDS

Come on, you children, gather around—
  Gather around, you children.
And we will lose that evil spirit
  Called the Voodoo.

Nothin' but trouble, if he has found,
  If he has found you, children—
  But you can chase the Hoodoo
  With the dance that you do.

  Let me lead the way.
  Jubilee today! Say!
He'll never hound you;
Stamp on the ground, you children!

Refrain

  Clap-a yo' hand! Slap-a yo' thigh!
    Halleluyah! Halleluyah!
Ev'rybody come along and join the Jubilee!

  Clap-a yo' hand! Slap-a yo' thigh!
  Don't you lose time! Don't you lose time!
  Come along—it's Shake Yo' Shoes Time
    Now for you and me!

On the sands of time
You are only a pebble;
Remember, trouble must be treated
Just like a rebel;
Send him to the Debble!

  Clap-a yo' hand! Slap-a yo' thigh!
    Halleluyah! Halleluyah!
Ev'rybody come along and join the Jubilee!

CLAP YO' HANDS

Music and Lyrics by
GEORGE GERSHWIN and IRA GERSHWIN

56

DO, DO, DO

He

I remember the bliss
Of that wonderful kiss.
  I know that a boy
  Could never have more joy
From any little miss.

She

I remember it quite;
'Twas a wonderful night.

He

Oh, how I'd adore it
If you would encore it. Oh—

Refrain

Do, do, do
What you've done, done, done
  Before, Baby.
Do, do, do
What I do, do, do
  Adore, Baby.

Let's try again,
Sigh again,
Fly again to heaven.
  Baby, see
  It's ABC—
I love you and you love me.

I know, know, know
What a beau, beau, beau
  Should do, Baby;
So don't, don't don't
Say it won't, won't, won't
  Come true, Baby.

My heart begins to hum—
Hum de dum de dum-dum-dum,
  So do, do, do
  What you've done, done, done
    Before.

She

Sweets we've tasted before,
Cannot stand an encore.
  You know that a miss
  Who always gives a kiss
Would soon become a bore.

He

I can't see that at all
True love should never pall.

She

I was only teasing
What you did was pleasing. Oh—

Refrain

Do, do, do
What you've done, done, done
  Before, Baby.
Do, do, do
What I do, do, do
  Adore, Baby.

Let's try again,
Sigh again,
Fly again to heaven.
  Baby, see
  It's ABC—
I love you and you love me.

He

You dear, dear, dear
little dear, dear, dear
  Come here, snappy
And see, see, see
little me, me, me
  Make you, happy.

She

My heart begins to sigh—
Di de di de di-di-di
  So do, do, do
  What you've done, done, done
    Before.

DO, DO, DO

Music and Lyrics by
GEORGE GERSHWIN and IRA GERSHWIN

'S WONDERFUL

He

Life has just begun:
Jack has found his Jill.
Don't know what you've done,
But I'm all a-thrill.
How can words express
Your divine appeal?
You could never guess
All the love I feel.
From now on, lady, I insist,
For me no other girls exist.

Refrain

'S wonderful! 'S marvelous—
    You should care for me!
'S awful nice! 'S Paradise—
    'S what I love to see!
You've made my life so glamorous,
You can't blame me for feeling amorous.
    Oh, 's wonderful! 'S marvelous—
    That you should care for me!

She

Don't mind telling you,
In my humble fash,
That you thrill me through
With a tender pash.
When you said you care,
'Magine my emosh;
I swore, then and there,
Permanent devosh.
You made all other boys seem blah;
Just you alone filled me with AAH!

Refrain

'S wonderful! 'S marvelous—
    You should care for me!
'S awful nice! 'S Paradise—
    'S what I love to see!
My dear, it's four leaf clover time;
From now on my heart's working overtime.
    Oh, 's wonderful! 'S marvelous—
    That you should care for me!

'S WONDERFUL

Music and Lyrics by
GEORGE GERSHWIN and IRA GERSHWIN

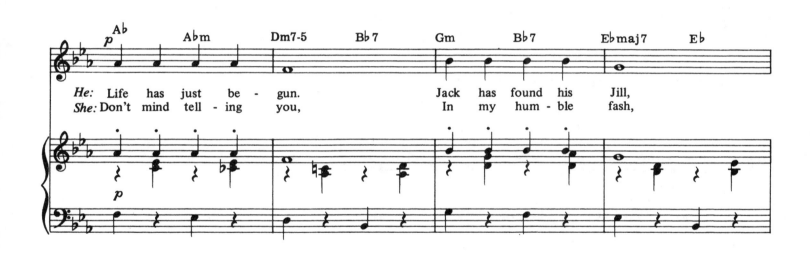

He: Life has just be - gun.   Jack has found his   Jill,
She: Don't mind tell - ing you,   In my hum - ble   fash,

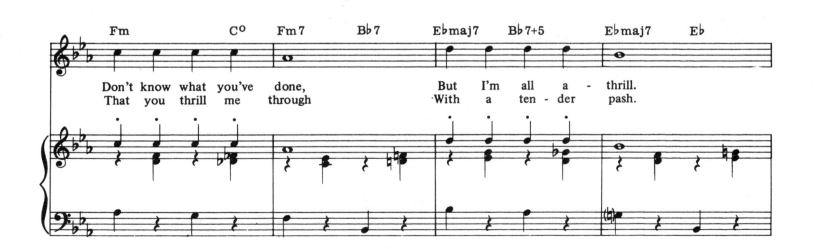

Don't know what you've done,   But I'm all a - thrill.
That you thrill me through   With a ten - der pash.

64

'S WONDERFUL

Third Refrain

'S magnifique!   (sman-nee-feek)
'S what I seek—   (swat)
You should care for me!

'S elegant!   (sell-a-ghant)
'S what I want!   (swat)
'S what I love to see!   (swat)
You've made my life so tinglish,   (tingle-ish)
I'll even overlook your English!   (engle-ish)
'Sexceptionnel!   (sex-ep-shun-el)
'S no Bagatelle—
That you should care for me!

STRIKE UP THE BAND

We fought in nineteen-seventeen,
  Rum-ta-ta tum-tum-tum!
And drove the tyrant from the scene,
  Rum-ta-ta tum-tum-tum!
We hope there'll be no other war
  But if we are forced into one—
The flag that we'll be fighting for,
  Is the Red and White and Blue One!
We do not favor war alarms
  Rum-ta-ta tum-tum-tum!
But if we hear the call to arms,
  Rum-ta-ta tum-tum-tum!
  Rum-ta-ta tum-tum-tum!
  Rum-ta-ta tum-tum-tum!

Refrain

Let the drums roll out!
  (Boom boom boom!)
Let the trumpet call!
  (Ta-ta-ra-ta-ta-ta-ta!)
While the people shout
  (Hooray!)
Strike up the bank!

Hear the cymbals ring!
  (Tszing-tszing-tszing!)
Calling one and all
  (Ta-ta-ra-ta-ta-ta-ta!)
To the martial swing,
  (Left, right!)
Strike up the band!

There is work to be done, to be done—
There's a war to be won, to be won—
Come you son of a gun—
  Take your stand!

  Fall in line, yea bo—
  Come along, let's go!
Hey, leader, STRIKE UP THE BAND!

Second Release

Yankee Doo, Doodle-oo, Doodle-oo—
We'll come through, Doodle-oo, Doodle-oo—
For the red, white and blue, Doodle-oo—
  Lend a hand!

  With our flag unfurled—
  For a brave, new world!
Hey, leader, STRIKE UP THE BAND!

STRIKE UP THE BAND

Music and Lyrics by
GEORGE GERSHWIN and IRA GERSHWIN

SOON

He

I'm making up for all the years
  That I waited;
  I'm compensated
    At last.
My heart is through with shirking;
Thanks to you it's working
    Fast.
The many lonely nights and days
  When this duffer
  Just had to suffer
    Are past.

Refrain

Soon—the lonely nights will be ended;
Soon—two hearts as one will be blended.
I've found the happiness I've waited for:
The only girl that I was fated for.
Oh! Soon—a little cottage will find us
Safe, with all our cares far behind us.
The day you're mine this world will be in tune.
Let's make that day come soon.

She

Soon—my dear, you'll never be lonely;
Soon—you'll find I live for you only.
When I'm with you who cares what time it is,
Or what the place or what the climate is?
Oh! Soon—our little ship will come sailing
Home, through every storm, never failing.
The day you're mine this world will be in tune.
Let's make that day come soon.

SOON

Music and Lyrics by
GEORGE GERSHWIN and IRA GERSHWIN

Moderato

He: I'm mak - ing up for all the years that I wait - ed, I'm com - pen - sat - ed at last.

My heart is through with shirk - ing, thanks to you it's work - ing

CHEERFUL LITTLE EARFUL

I'm growing tired of, lovey dove theme songs,
That fifty million pianos pound.
And in an age where these, Radios scream songs,
I only want one phrase around me—

Refrain

There's a cheerful little earful
Gosh I miss it something fearful
and this cheerful little earful—
Is the well known "I love you."
Stocks can go down, bus'ness slow down
But the milk and honey
Flow down with a cheerful little earful—
Of the well known "I love you".
In ev'ry play it's a set phrase,
What the public get phrase.
But as a pet phrase
It'll do do do

Poopa roo-it soft and cu-it,
Make me happy you can do it,
With a cheerful little earful—
Of the well known "I love you".

CHEERFUL LITTLE EARFUL

Words by
IRA GERSHWIN and BILLY ROSE

Music by
HARRY WARREN

VOICE

I'm grow-ing tir-ed of lov-ey dove theme songs

That fif-ty mil-lion pia-nos pound

CHORUS

BUT NOT FOR ME

Old Man Sunshine—listen, you!
Never tell me Dreams Come True!
   Just try it—
  And I'll start a riot.
Beatrice Fairfax—don't you dare
Ever tell me he will care;
   I'm certain
  It's the Final Curtain.
  I never want to hear
  From any cheer-
   Ful Pollyannas,
  Who tell you Fate
  Supplies a Mate—
   It's all bananas!

Refrain

They're writing songs of love,
   But not for me;
A lucky star's above,
   But not for me.

With Love to Lead the Way,
I've found more Clouds of Gray
Than any Russian play
   Could guarantee.

I was a fool to fall
   And Get That Way;
Heigh ho! Alas! and al-
   So, Lackaday!

Although I can't dismiss
The mem'ry of his kiss—
   I guess he's not for me.

Second Refrain

He's knocking on a door,
   But not for me;
He'll plan a two by four,
   But not for me.

I know that Love's a Game;
I'm puzzled just the same—
Was I the Moth or Flame ...?
   I'm all at sea.

It all began so well,
   But what an end!
This is the time a Fell-
   Er Needs a Friend:

When ev'ry happy plot
Ends with the marriage knot—
   And there's no knot for me.

BUT NOT FOR ME

Music and Lyrics by
GEORGE GERSHWIN and IRA GERSHWIN

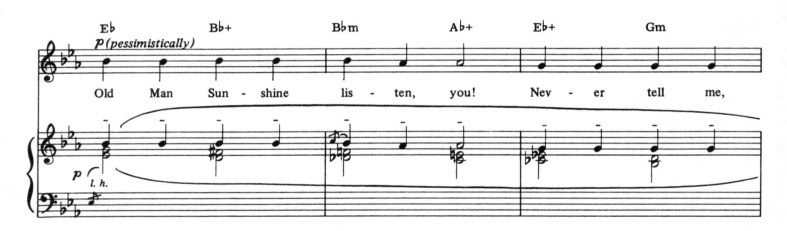

Old Man Sun - shine lis - ten, you! Nev - er tell me,

"Dreams come true!" Just try it And I'll start a ri - ot._____

I'VE GOT A CRUSH ON YOU

He

How glad the many millions
of Annabelles and Lillians
  Would be
  To capture me
But you had such persistence
You wore down my resistance;
  I fell—
  And it was swell.

She

You're my big and brave and handsome Romeo.
How I won you I shall never, never know.

He

It's not that you're attractive—
But oh, my heart grew active
  When you
  Came into view.

Refrain

I've got a crush on you,
  Sweetie Pie.
All the day and nighttime
  Hear me sigh.
I never had the least notion
That I could fall with so much emotion.

  Could you coo,
  Could you care
For a cunning cottage we could share?
  The world will pardon my mush
  'Cause I've got a crush,
  My baby, on you.

She

How glad a million laddies
From millionaires to caddies
  Would be
  To capture me
But you had such persistence
You wore down my resistance;
  I fell—
  And it was swell.

You're my big and brave and handsome Romeo.
How you won me I shall never, never know.

It's not that you're attractive—
But oh, my heart grew active
  When you
  Came into view.

Refrain

I've got a crush on you,
  Sweetie Pie.
All the day and nighttime
  Hear me sigh.
This isn't just a flirtation:
We're proving that there's predestination.

  I could coo,
  I could care
For that cunning cottage we could share.
  Your mush I never shall shush
  'Cause I've got a crush,
  My baby, on you.

I'VE GOT A CRUSH ON YOU

Music and Lyrics by
GEORGE GERSHWIN and IRA GERSHWIN

wore down my re-sist-ance: I fell, _____ and it was swell. _____

She: You're my big and brave and hand-some Ro-me-o. How I

won you I shall nev-er, nev-er know. *He:* It's not that you're at-trac-tive, But

BIDIN' MY TIME

1

Some fellers love to Tip-Toe Through The Tulips;
Some fellers go on Singing In The Rain;
Some fellers keep on Paintin' Skies With Sunshine;
Some fellers keep on Swingin' Down The Lane—
                                        But—

Refrain

I'm Bidin' My Time,
  'Cause that's the kinda guy I'm.
While other folks grow dizzy
I keep busy—
    Bidin' My Time.

Next year, next year,
Somethin's bound to happen;
  This year, this year,
I'll just keep on nappin'—

And—Bidin' My Time,
'Cause that's the kinda guy I'm.
  There's no regrettin'
  When I'm settin'—
  Bidin' My Time.

2

Some fellers love to Tell It To The Daisies;
Some Stroll Beneath The Honeysuckle Vines;
Some fellers when they've Climbed The Highest Mountain
Still keep a-Cryin' For The Carolines—
                                        But—

Refrain

I'm Bidin' My Time,
  'Cause that's the kinda guy I'm—
Beginnin' on a Mond'y
Right through Sund'y,
    Bidin' My Time.

Give me, give me
(A) glass that's full of tinkle;
  Let me, let me
Dream like Rip Van Winkle.

He Bided His Time,
And like that Winkle guy I'm.
  Chasin' 'way flies,
  How the day flies—
  Bidin' My Time!

BIDIN' MY TIME

Music and Lyrics by
GEORGE GERSHWIN and IRA GERSHWIN

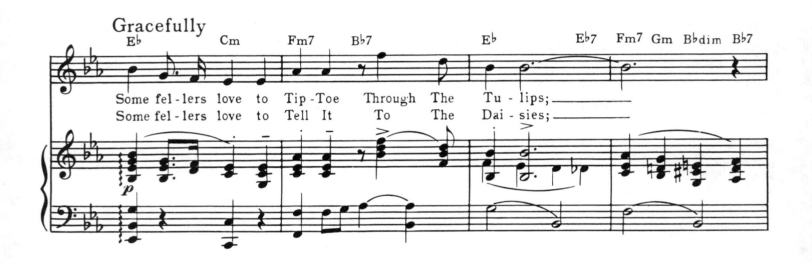

Some fel-lers love to Tip-Toe Through The Tu-lips;
Some fel-lers love to Tell It To The Dai-sies;

Some fel-lers go on Sing - ing In The Rain.
Some Stroll Be-neath The Hon - ey-suc-kle Vines;

EMBRACEABLE YOU

He

Dozens of girls would storm up;
  I had to lock my door.
Somehow I couldn't warm up
  To one before.
What was it that controlled me?
  What kept my love-life lean?
My intuition told me
  You'd come on the scene.
Lady, listen to the rhythm of my heart beat,
  And you'll get just what I mean.

Refrain

  Embrace me,
My sweet embraceable you.
  Embrace me,
 You irreplaceable you.
Just one look at you—my heart grew tipsy in me;
You and you alone bring out the gypsy in me.
  I love all
The many charms about you;
  Above all
I want my arms about you.
Don't be a naughty baby,
Come to papa—come to papa—do!
My sweet embraceable you.

She

I went about reciting,
  "Here's one who'll never fall!"
But I'm afraid the writing
  Is on the wall.
My nose I used to turn up

When you'd besiege my heart;
Now I completely burn up
  When you're slow to start.
I'm afraid you'll have to take the consequences;
  You upset the apple cart.

Refrain

  Embrace me,
My sweet embraceable you.
  Embrace me,
You irreplaceable you.
In your arms I find love so delectable, dear,
I'm afraid it isn't quite respectable, dear.
  But hang it—
Come on, let's glorify love!
  Ding dang it!
You'll shout "Encore!" if I love.
Don't be a naughty papa,
Come to baby—come to baby—do!
My sweet embraceable you.

Third Refrain

  Dear lady,
My silk and laceable you,
  Dear lady,
Be my embraceable you.
You're the only one I love, yes, verily so!
But you're much too shy, unnecessarily so!
  I'll try not
To be so formal, my dear;
  Am I not
A man who's normal, my dear?
There's just one way to cheer me;
Come to papa—come to papa, do!
My sweet embraceable you.

EMBRACEABLE YOU

Music and Lyrics by
GEORGE GERSHWIN and IRA GERSHWIN

What was it that con-trolled me? What kept my love-life lean?
My nose I used to turn up When you'd be-siege my heart;

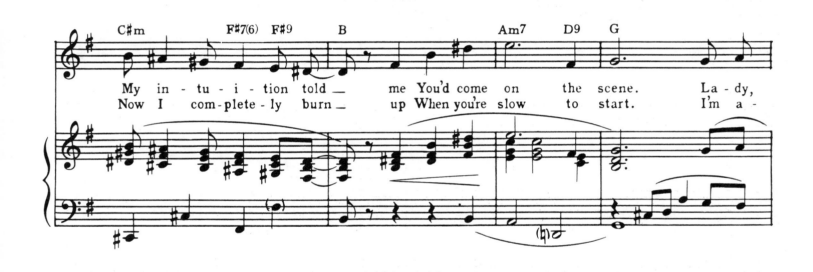

My in-tu-i-tion told me You'd come on the scene. La-dy,
Now I com-plete-ly burn up When you're slow to start. I'm a-

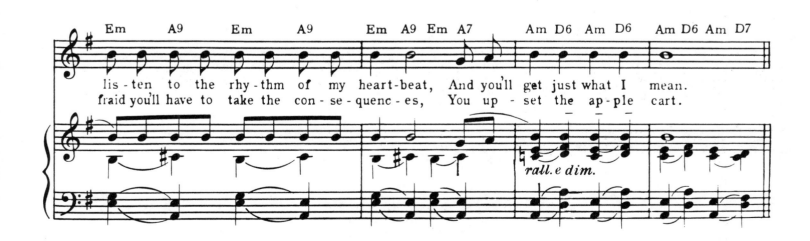

lis-ten to the rhy-thm of my heart-beat, And you'll get just what I mean.
fraid you'll have to take the con-se-quenc-es, You up-set the ap-ple cart.

Refrain *(rhythmically, but not fast)*

EMBRACEABLE YOU

Reprise
She

   You call me
Your sweet embraceable you
   You call me
Your irreplaceable you—
When you talk that way it's so delectable, dear,
I'm afraid it isn't quite respectable, dear.
   When you, sir,
Act so deliriously,
   Then who, sir,
Could take you seriously?
There's no one I'm more fond of,
But I don't see any hurry to
Be your embraceable you.

I GOT RHYTHM

Days can be sunny,
  With never a sigh;
Don't need what money
  Can buy.

Birds in the tree sing
  Their dayful of song.
Why shouldn't we sing
  Along?

I'm chipper all the day,
  Happy with my lot.
How do I get that way?
  Look at what I've got:

Refrain

I got rhythm,
I got music,
I got my man—
Who could ask for anything more?

I got daisies
In green pastures,
I got my man—
Who could ask for anything more?

Old Man Trouble
I don't mind him—
You won't find him
  'Round my door.

I got starlight
I got sweet dreams
I got my man—
Who could ask for anything more—
Who could ask for anything more?

I GOT RHYTHM

Music and Lyrics by
GEORGE GERSHWIN and IRA GERSHWIN

105

REFRAIN (*with abandon*)

WHO CARES
(SO LONG AS YOU CARE FOR ME)

Let it rain and thunder!
Let a million firms go under!
I am not concerned with—
      Stocks and bonds that I've been burned with.

I love you and you love me
And that's how it will always be—
And nothing else
      Can ever mean a thing.

Who cares what the public chatters?
Love's the only thing that matters.

Refrain

      Who cares
If the sky cares to fall in the sea?
Who cares what banks fail in Yonkers
Long as you've got a kiss that conquers?
      Why should I care?
Life is one long jubilee
So long as I care for you—
And you care for me.

Alternate Release:

Who cares how history rates me?
Long as your kiss intoxicates me!

WHO CARES
(SO LONG AS YOU CARE FOR ME)

Music and Lyrics by
GEORGE GERSHWIN and IRA GERSHWIN

Let it rain and thun-der! Let a mil-lion

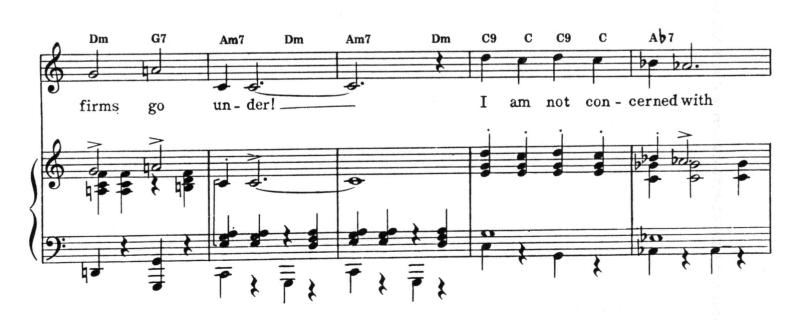

firms go un-der! I am not con-cerned with

Refrain

(in a lilting manner)

OF THEE I SING

From the Island of Manhattan to the Coast of Gold,
   From North to South, from East to West,
   You are the love I love the best.
You're the dream girl of the sweetest story ever told;
   A dream I've sought both night andy day
   For years through all the U.S.A.
  The star I've hitched my wagon to
  Is very obviously you.

Refrain

   Of thee I sing, baby—
Summer, autumn, winter, spring, baby.
   You're my silver lining,
   You're my sky of blue;
   There's a lovelight shining
   Just because of you.

   Of thee I sing, baby—
You have got that certain thing, baby!
   Shining star and inspiration,
   Worthy of a mighty nation—
     Of thee I sing!

OF THEE I SING

Music and Lyrics by
GEORGE GERSHWIN and IRA GERSHWIN

From the Is-land of Man-hat-tan to the Coast of Gold, From North to South, From East to West, You are the love I love the best.

LOVE IS SWEEPING THE COUNTRY

Why are people gay
  All the night and day,
Feeling as they never felt before?
  What is the thing?
  That makes them sing?

  Rich man, poor man, thief,
  Doctor, lawyer, chief
Feel a feeling that they can't ignore;
  It plays a part
  In ev'ry heart,
And ev'ry heart is shouting "Encore!"

  Refrain

Love is sweeping the country;
Waves are hugging the shore;
  All the sexes
  From Maine to Texas
Have never known such love before.

See them billing and cooing
Like the birdies above!
  Girl and boy alike,
  Sharing joy alike,
  Feel that passion'll
  Soon be national.
Love is sweeping the country—
There never was so much love!

LOVE IS SWEEPING THE COUNTRY

Music and Lyrics by
GEORGE GERSHWIN and IRA GERSHWIN

BLAH, BLAH, BLAH

I've written you a song,
A beautiful routine;
(I hope you like it.)
My technique can't be wrong:
I learned it from the screen.
(I hope you like it.)
I studied all the rhymes that all the lovers sing;
Then just for you I wrote this little thing.

Refrain

Blah, blah, blah, blah, moon,
Blah, blah, blah, above;
Blah, blah, blah, blah, croon,
Blah, blah, blah, blah, love.
Tra la la la, merry month of May;
Tra la la la, 'neath the clouds of gray.
Blah, blah, blah, your hair,
Blah, blah, blah, your eyes;
Blah, blah, blah, blah, care,
Blah, blah, blah, blah, skies.
Tra la la la, tra la la la la, cottage for two—
Blah, blah, blah, blah, blah, darling with you!

BLAH, BLAH, BLAH

Music and Lyrics by
GEORGE GERSHWIN and IRA GERSHWIN

MINE

John

My good friends, don't praise me!
I owe it all to the little woman,
This little woman, *my* little woman.

All

His little woman.

John

She's the reason for my success,
Why, when I think how we suffered together—
Worried together, struggled together,
Stood together together,
I grow so sentimental I'm afraid
I've got to burst into song

All

Please do!
We'd love to know how you feel about her
And how she feels about you.

Refrain (John)

Mine, love is mine,
Whether it rain or storm or shine.
Mine, you are mine,
Never another valentine.
And I am yours,
Tell me that I'm yours;
Show me that smile my heart adores.
Mine, more than divine,
To know that love like yours is mine!

Patter
(First Time Sung Solo, Repeat Second Time With Chorus)

The point they're making in the song
Is that they more than get along;
And he is not ashamed to say
She made him what he is today.
It does a person good to see
Such happy domesticity;
The way they're making love you'd swear
They're not a married pair.
He says, no matter what occurs,
Whatever he may have is hers;
The point that *she* is making is—
Whatever *she* may have is his.
Mine, more than divine,
To know that love like yours is mine!

MINE

Music and Lyrics by
GEORGE GERSHWIN and IRA GERSHWIN

SWEET SO AND SO

He

I knew, my dear, from the moment that we met,
    deep in my heart I'd install you;
Hoping the love song would soon be a duet
    I dreamed of pet names to call you.
    I looked in my thesaurus—
      And there I found a few;
    I'll sing a little chorus—
      Of pet names meant for you:

Refrain

You darling, you ducky,
    You sweet so and so;
You sweet thing you neat thing,
    You've set me aglow.
My heaven, my rapture,
    My sweet this and that,
Without you my life would be flat.
Oh, I've a million more terms of endearment,
If you'll agree that for each other we're meant.
  My Venus, my goddess
    Let me be your beau,
And'll you'll be my sweet so and so.

She

All those impassioned avowels you have made,
    Those tender pet names you've chosen
Have broken down my resistance I'm afraid.
    You'd melt a heart that was frozen.
    Oh, how could I be chilly,
      You've thrilled me thru and thru;
    Tho' pet names may be silly
      I've lots reserved for you:

Refrain

My brave man, my cave man,
    My sweet so and so;
My mopsy, my popsy,
    My great Romeo!
My Pierrot, my hero,
    My sweet this and that,
You're making my heart pit a pat.
I never knew you had such romance in you;
You've got a sporting chance if you continue.
    Oh laddie! Oh daddy!
      In time I may grow
To love you, you sweet so and so.

SWEET SO AND SO

Words by
IRA GERSHWIN

Music by
JOSEPH MEYER and PHILIP CHARIG

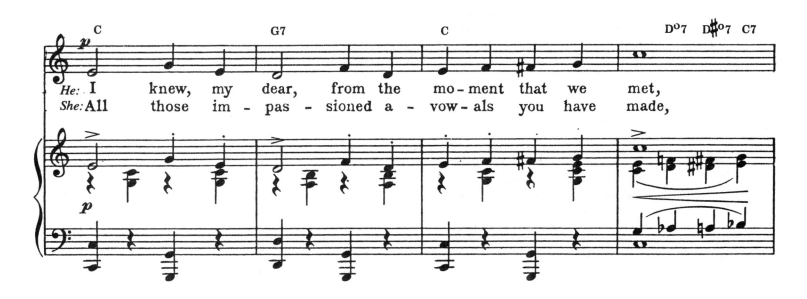

He: I knew, my dear, from the mo-ment that we met,
She: All those im-pas-sioned a-vow-als you have made,

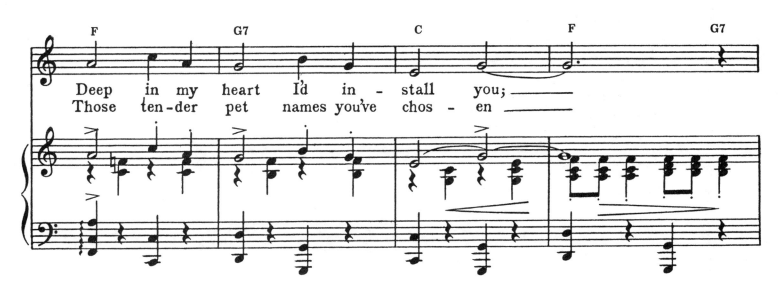

Deep in my heart I'd in-stall you; ____
Those ten-der pet names you've chos-en ____

I GOT PLENTY O' NUTHIN'

Oh, I got plenty o' nuthin'
An' nuthin's plenty fo' me.
I got no car, got no mule, I got no misery.
De folks wid plenty o' plenty
Got a lock on dey door,
'Fraid somebody's a-goin' to rob 'em
While dey's out a-makin' more.
What for?
I got no lock on de door,
(Dat's no way to be).
Dey can steal de rug from de floor,
Dat's O.K. wid me,
'Cause de things dat I prize,
Like de stars in de skies,
All are free,
Oh, I got plenty o' nuthin'
An' nuthin's plenty fo' me.
I got my gal, got my song,
Got Hebben de whole day long.
(No use complainin'!)
Got my gal, got my Lawd, got my song.

I got plenty o' nuthin'
An' nuthin's plenty fo' me.
I got de sun, got de moon, got de deep blue sea.
De folks wid plenty o' plenty
Got to pray all de day.
Seems wid plenty you sure got to worry
How to keep de Debble away,
A-way
I ain't a-frettin' 'bout Hell
Till de time arrive.
Never worry long as I'm well,
Never one to strive
To be good, to be bad—
What the hell! I is glad
I's alive
Oh, I got plenty o' nuthin'
An' nuthin's plenty fo' me.
I got my gal, got my song,
Got Hebben de whole day long.
(No use complainin'!)
Got my gal, got my Lawd, got my song.

I GOT PLENTY O' NUTHIN'

Words and Music by GEORGE GERSHWIN,
DU BOSE and DOROTHY HEYWARD and IRA GERSHWIN

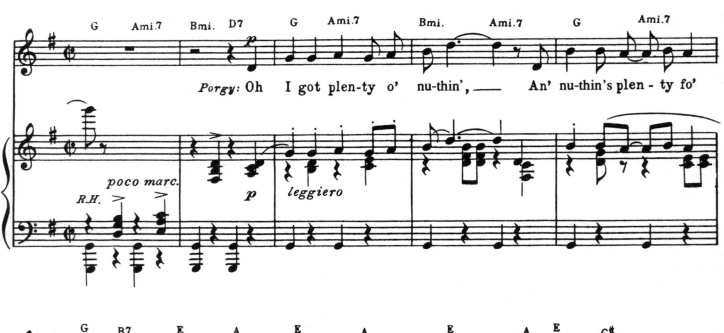

I CAN'T GET STARTED
(STANDARD VERSION)

I'm a glum one; it's explainable:
I met someone unattainable.
    Life's a bore,
The world is my oyster no more.
All the papers, where I led the news
With my capers, now will spread the news:
    "Superman
Turns out to be Flash In The Pan!"

First Refrain

I've flown arond the world in a plane;
I've settled revolutions in Spain;
    The North Pole I have charted—
    But can't get started with you.

Around a golf course I'm under par
And all the movies want me to star;
    I've got a house—a show place,
    But I get no place with you.

    You're so supreme—
Lyrics I write of you,
    Scheme
Just for a sight of you,
    Dream—
Both day and night of you—
And what good does it do?

In nineteen twenty nine I sold short;
In England I'm presented at court.
    But you've got me down-hearted
    'Cause I can't get started with you.

Second Refrain

I do a hundred yards in ten flat;
The Prince of Wales has copied my hat;
    With queens I've a la carted—
    But can't get started with you.

The leading tailors follow my styles,
And toothpaste ads all feature my smiles;
    The Astorbilts I visit—
    But say, what *is* it—with you.

    When first we met—
How you elated me!
    Pet!
You devastated me!
    Yet—
Now you've deflated me
Till you're my Waterloo.

I've sold my kisses at a bazaar—
And after me they've named a cigar,
    But lately how I've smarted
    'Cause I can't get started with you.

I CAN'T GET STARTED
(VERSION FOR FRANK SINATRA)

I'm a glum one; it's explainable:
I met someone unattainable.
　　Life's a bore,
The world is my oyster no more.
All the papers, where I led the news
With my capers, now will spread the news:
　　"Superman
Turns out to be Flash In The Pan!"

First Refrain

I've flown through outer space in a plane;
I've made the moon my secret domain.
　The Russians I've outsmarted—
　But can't get started with you.

All the Olympic medals I've won
Prove my physique is second to none;
　My heart is big and roomy
　What good's it *do* me with you.

　　When first we met—
How you elated me!
　　Pet!
You devastated me!
　　Yet—
Now you've deflated me
Till you're my Waterloo.

In Cincinnati or in Rangoon
I smile and gals go into a swoon;
　But you've got me down-hearted
　'Cause I can't get started with you.

Second Refrain

I'm written up in *Fortune* and *Time;*
The biggest and the latest news, I'm.
　For me they strike the band up . . . .
　I'm just a stand-up with you.

*D'you know the Texas taxes I pay?
(I gush a million barrels a day).
　Each house I own's a show place
　But I get no place with you.

　　Oh, tell me why
Am I no kick to you—
　　I,
Who'd always stick to you.
　　Fly—
Through thick and thin to you?
Tell me why I'm taboo!

I offer you a man among mice—
(I could have been the President twice!)
　With queens I've a la carted—
　But I can't get started with you.

*NOTE FROM THE AUTHOR:
　An excellent substitute for this stanza:

I'm welcomed anywhere I may be;
Why, Greta Garbo's had me to tea.
　The Ira Gershwins I visit,
　But, say, what *is* it with you?

I CAN'T GET STARTED

Words by
IRA GERSHWIN

Music by
VERNON DUKE

I'm a glum one, it's ex-plain-a-ble: I met some one un-at-tain-a-ble;

Life's a-bore, The world is my oy-ster no more.

All the pa-pers where I led the news With my ca-pers now will spread the news,

"Su - per - man Turns Out To Be Flash In The Pan!"

Refrain

I've flown a - round the world in a plane;_ I've set - tled re - vo - lu - tions in
(I do a) hun-dred yards in ten flat;_ The Prince of Wales has cop - ied my

Spain; The North Pole I have char - ted, But can't get start - ed with
hat; With queens I've à la cart - ed,_ But can't get start - ed with

I CAN'T GET STARTED
(FEMALE VERSION)

I'm a glum one; it's explainable:
I met someone unattainable.
    Life's a bore,
The world is my oyster no more.
All the papers, where I led the news
With my capers, now will spread the news:
    "Super Gal
Is Punchy and Losing Morale!"

First Refrain

When I sell kisses at a bazaar,
The wolves line up from nearby and far;
   With king I've a la carted—
   But can't get started with you.

The millionaires I've had to turn down
Would stretch from London to New York Town;
   The upper crust I visit,
   But say, what *is* it—with you?

    When first we met—
How you elated me!
    Pet!
You devestated me!
    Yet—
Now you've deflated me
Till you're my Waterloo.

Though beauty columns ask my advice,
Though I was "Miss America" twice,
   Still you've got me outsmarted
   'Cause I can't get started with you.

Second Refrain

The Himalaya Mountains I climb;
I'm written up in *Fortune* and *Time*.
   I dig the 4th Dimension,
   But no attention from you!

There's always "Best regards and much love"
From Mr. Dewey—you know, the Gov;
   I'm there at every State Ball
   But behind the 8-ball with you.

    Oh, tell me why
Am I no kick to you—
    I,
Who'd always stick to you.
    Fly—
Through thick and thin to you?
Tell me why I'm taboo!

The market trembles when I sell short;
In England I'm presented at court.
   The Siamese Twins I've parted—
   But I can't get started with you.

A FOGGY DAY
(IN LONDON TOWN)

I was a stranger in the city.
    Out of town were the people I knew.
I had that feeling of self-pity:
    What to do? What to do? What to do?
    The outlook was decidedly blue.
But as I walked through the foggy streets alone,
It turned out to be the luckiest day I've known.

Refrain

A foggy day in London Town
Had me low and had me down.
I viewed the morning with alarm.
The British Museum had lost its charm.
How long, I wondered, could this thing last?
But the age of miracles hadn't passed,
For, suddenly, I saw you there—
And through foggy London Town
The sun was shining ev'rywhere.

A FOGGY DAY
(IN LONDON TOWN)

Music and Lyrics by
GEORGE GERSHWIN and IRA GERSHWIN

I was a strang-er in the cit-y.___ Out of town were the peo-ple I knew.

I had that feel-ing of self - pi-ty,___ What to do? What to do? What to do? The

THEY CAN'T TAKE THAT AWAY FROM ME

Our romance won't end on a sorrowful note,
    Though by tomorrow you're gone;
The song is ended, but as the songwriter wrote,
    "The melody lingers on."
  They may take you from me,
    I'll miss your fond caress.
  But though they take you from me,
    I'll still possess:

      Refrain

  The way you wear your hat,
    The way you sip your tea,
  The mem'ry of all that—
No, no! They can't take that away from me!

  The way your smile just beams,
    The way you sing off key,
  The way you haunt my dreams—
No, no! They can't take that away from me!

  We may never, never meet again
    On the bumpy road to love,
  Still I'll always, always keep
    The mem'ry of—

  The way you hold your knife,
    They way we danced till three,
  The way you've changed my life—
No, no! They can't take away from me!
No! They can't take that away from me!

THEY CAN'T TAKE THAT AWAY FROM ME

Music and Lyrics by
GEORGE GERSHWIN and **IRA GERSHWIN**

THEY ALL LAUGHED

The odds were a hundred to one against me,
The world thought the heights were too high to climb.
But people from Missouri never incensed me:
  Oh, I wasn't a bit concerned,
  For from hist'ry I had learned
  How many, many times the worm had turned.

Refrain

They all laughed at Christopher Columbus
When he said the world was round;
They all laughed when Edison recorded sound.

They all laughed at Wilbur and his brother
  When they said that man could fly;
    They told Marconi
    Wireless was a phony—
  It's the same old cry!

They laughed at me wanting you,
  Said I was reaching for the moon;
But oh, you came through—
  Now, they'll have to change their tune.

They all said we never could be happy,
  They laughed at us—and how!
    But ho, ho, ho—
  Who's got the last laugh now?

Second Refrain

They all laughed at Rockefeller Center—
Now they're fighting to get in;
They all laughed at Whitney and his cotton gin.

They all laughed at Fulton and his steamboat,
  Hershey and his choc'late bar.
    Ford and his Lizzie
    Kept the laughers busy—
  That's how people are!

They laughed at me wanting you—
  Said it would be Hello! Good-bye!
But oh, you came through—
  Now they're eating humble pie.

They all said we'd never get together—
  Darling, let's take a bow,
    For ho, ho, ho—
  Who's got the last laugh—
    He, he, he—
  Let's at the past laugh—
    Ha, ha, ha—
  Who's got the last laugh now?

THEY ALL LAUGHED

Music and Lyrics by
GEORGE GERSHWIN and IRA GERSHWIN

The odds were a hun-dred to one a-gainst me. The world thought the heights were too high to climb. But

They told Mar-co-ni Wire-less was a pho-ney;
Ford and his Liz-zie Kept the laugh-ers bus-y;

It's the same old cry. They laughed at me____ want-ing
That's how peo-ple are. They laughed at me____ want-ing

you,____ Said I was reach-ing for the moon; But
you,____ Said it would be Hel-lo, Good-bye; But

oh,____ You came through__ Now they'll have to change their tune.
oh,____ You came through__ Now they're eat-ing hum-ble pie.

LET'S CALL THE WHOLE THING OFF

Things have come to a pretty pass—
   Our romance is growing flat,
For you like this and the other,
   While I go for this and that.
Goodness knows what the end will be;
   Oh, I don't know where I'm at . . . .
It looks as if we two will never be one.
Something must be done.

Refrain

You say eether and I say eyether,
You say neether and I say nyther;
Eether, eyether, neether, nyther—
   Let's call the whole thing off!

You like potato and I like po-tah-to,
You like tomato and I like to-mah-to;
Potato, po-tah-to, tomato, to-mah-to—
   Let's call the whole thing off!

But oh, if we call the whole thing off, then we must part.
And oh, if we ever part, then that might break my heart.

So, if you like pajamas and I like pa-jah-mas,
I'll wear pajamas and give up pa-jah-mas.
   For we know we
   Need each other, so we
Better call the calling off off.
Let's call the whole thing off!

Second Refrain

You say laughter and I say lawfter,
You say after and I say awfter;
Laughter, lawfter, after, awfter—
   Let's call the whole thing off!

You like vanilla and I like vanella,
You, sa's'parilla and I sa's'parella;
Vanilla, vanella, choc'late, strawb'ry—
   Let's call the whole thing off!

But oh, if we call the whole thing off, then we must part.
And oh, if we ever part, then that might break my heart.

So, if you for oysters and I go for ersters,
I'll order oysters and cancel the ersters.
   For we know we
   Need each other, so we
Better call the calling off off.
Let's call the whole thing off!

LET'S CALL THE WHOLE THING OFF

Music and Lyrics by
GEORGE GERSHWIN and IRA GERSHWIN

Things have come to a pret-ty pass, Our ro-mance is grow-ing flat, For

you like this and the oth-er__ While I go for this and that.

LET'S CALL THE WHOLE THING OFF

Third Refrain

I say father and you say pater,
I say mother and you say mater;
Father, mother, auntie, uncle—
  Let's call the whole thing off!

I like banana and you like ba-nahn-ah;
I say Havana and I get Ha-vahn-ah—
Banana, ba-nahn-ah, Havana, Ha-vahn-ah—
  Never a happy medium!

But oh, if we call the whole thing off, then we must part.
And oh, if we ever part, then that might break my heart.

So, if I go for scallops and you go for lobster,
No more discussion—we both order lobster.
  For we know we
  Need each other, so we
Better call the calling off off.
Let's call the whole thing off!

LOVE WALKED IN

Nothing seemed to matter anymore;
Didn't care what I was headed for.
  Time was standing still;
  Nothing counted till,
There came a knock-knock-knocking at the door.

Refrain

  Love walked right in
And drove the shadows away;
  Love walked right in
And brought my sunniest day.

  One magic moment,
And my heart seemed to know
  That love said "Hello!"—
Though not a word was spoken.

  One look, and I
Forgot the gloom of the past;
  One look, and I
Had found my future at last.

  One look, and I
Had found a world completely new,
When love walked in with you.

LOVE WALKED IN

Music and Lyrics by
GEORGE GERSHWIN and IRA GERSHWIN

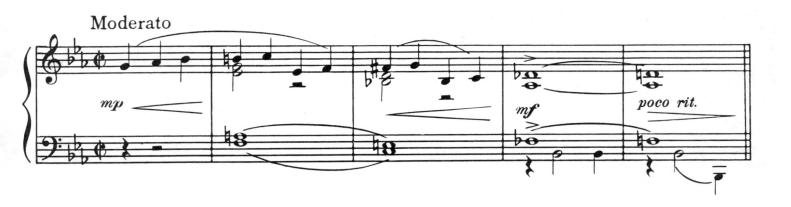

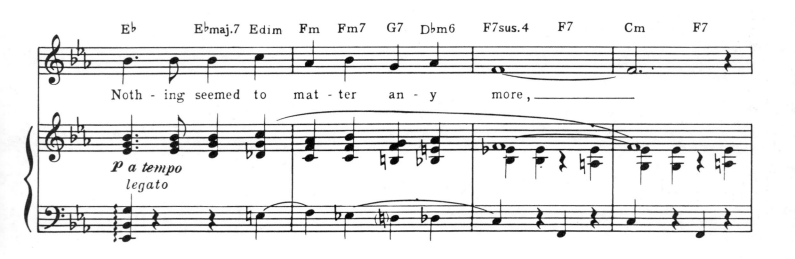

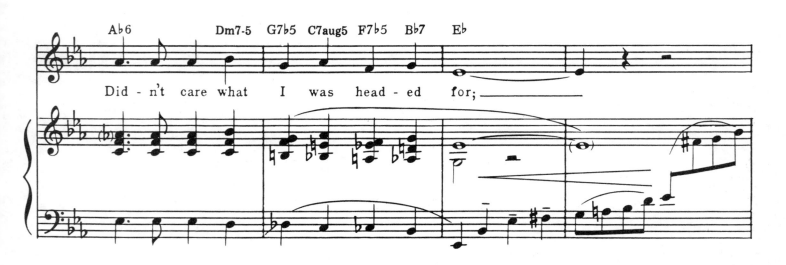

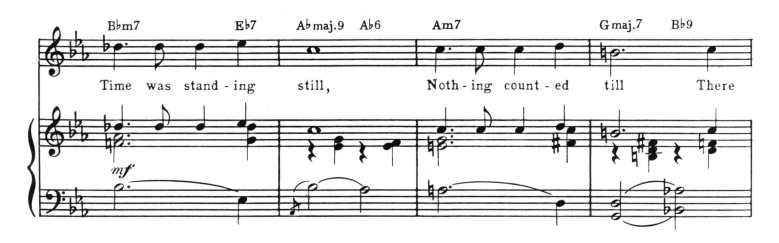

Time was stand-ing still, Noth-ing count-ed till There

came a knock-knock-knock-ing at the door. ____

Refrain *(slowly, with much expression)*

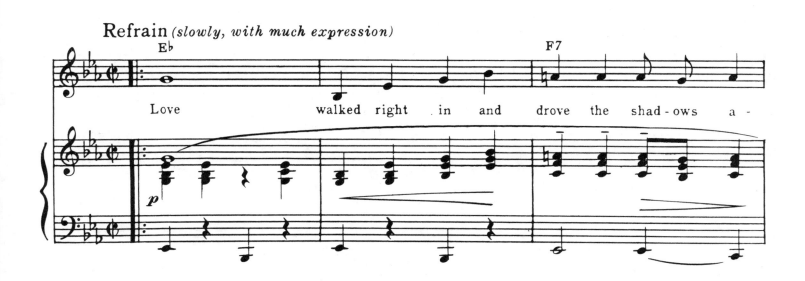

Love walked right in and drove the shad-ows a-

LOVE IS HERE TO STAY

The more I read the papers,
  The less I comprehend
The world and all its capers
  And how it all will end.
Nothing seems to be lasting,
  But that isn't our affair;
We've got something permanent—
  I mean, in the way we care.

Refrain

  It's very clear
Our love is here to stay;
  Not for a year,
But ever and a day.

The radio and the telephone
And the movies that we know
May just be passing fancies—
And in time may go.

  But oh, my dear,
Our love is here to stay.
  Together we're
Going a long, long way.

In time the Rockies may crumble,
Gibraltar may tumble
(They're only made of clay),
But—our love is here to stay.

LOVE IS HERE TO STAY

Music and Lyrics by
GEORGE GERSHWIN and IRA GERSHWIN

THE SAGA OF JENNY

There once was a girl named Jenny
Whose virtues were varied and many—
Excepting that she was inclined
Always to make up her mind;
And Jenny points a moral
With which you cannot quarrel
    As you will find.

Refrain

Jenny made her mind up when she was three
She, herself, was going to trim the Christmas tree.
Christmas Eve she lit the candles—tossed the taper away.
Little Jenny was an orphan on Christmas Day.

    Poor Jenny! Bright as a penny!
    Her equal would be hard to find.
        She lost one dad and mother,
        A sister and a brother—
        But she would make up her mind.

Jenny made her mind up when she was twelve
That into foreign langages she would delve;
But at seventeen to Vassar it was quite a blow
That in twenty-seven languages she couldn't say no.

    Poor Jenny! Bright as a penny!
    Her equal would be hard to find.
        To Jenny I'm beholden,
        He heart was big and golden,
        But she would make up her mind.

Jenny made her mind up at twenty-two
To get herself a husband was the thing to do.
She got herself all dolled up in her satins and furs
And she got herself a husband—but he wasn't hers.

    Poor Jenny! Bright as a penny!
    Her equal would be hard to find.
        Deserved a bed of roses,
        But history discloses,
        That she would make up her mind.

Jenny made her mind up at thrity-nine
She would take a trip to the Argentine.
She was only on vacation but the Latins agree
Jenny was the one who started the Good Neighbor Policy.

    Poor Jenny! Bright as a penny!
    Her equal would be hard to find.
       Oh, passion doesn't vanish
       In Portuguese or Spanish
    But she would make up her mind.

Jenny made her mind up at fifty-one
She would write her memoirs before she was done.
The very day her book was published, hist'ry relates
There were wives who shot their husbands in some
   thirty-three states.

    Poor Jenny! Bright as a penny!
    Her equal would be hard to find.
       She could give cards and spade-ies
       To many other ladies—
    But she would make up her mind.

Jenny made her mind up at seventy-five
She would live to be the oldest woman alive.
But gin and rum and destiny play funny tricks,
And poor Jenny kicked the bucket a seventy-six.

    Jenny points a moral
    With which you cannot quarrel.
  Makes a lot of common sense!

    Jenny and her saga
    Prove that you are gaga
If you don't keep sitting on the fence.

    Jenny and her story
    Point the way to glory
To all men and womankind.

    Anyone with vision
    Comes to this decision:
Don't make up—You shouldn't make up—
You mustn't make up—Oh, never make up—
    Anyone with vision
    Comes to this decison:
DON'T MAKE UP YOUR MIND!

THE SAGA OF JENNY

Lyrics by
IRA GERSHWIN

Music by
KURT WEILL

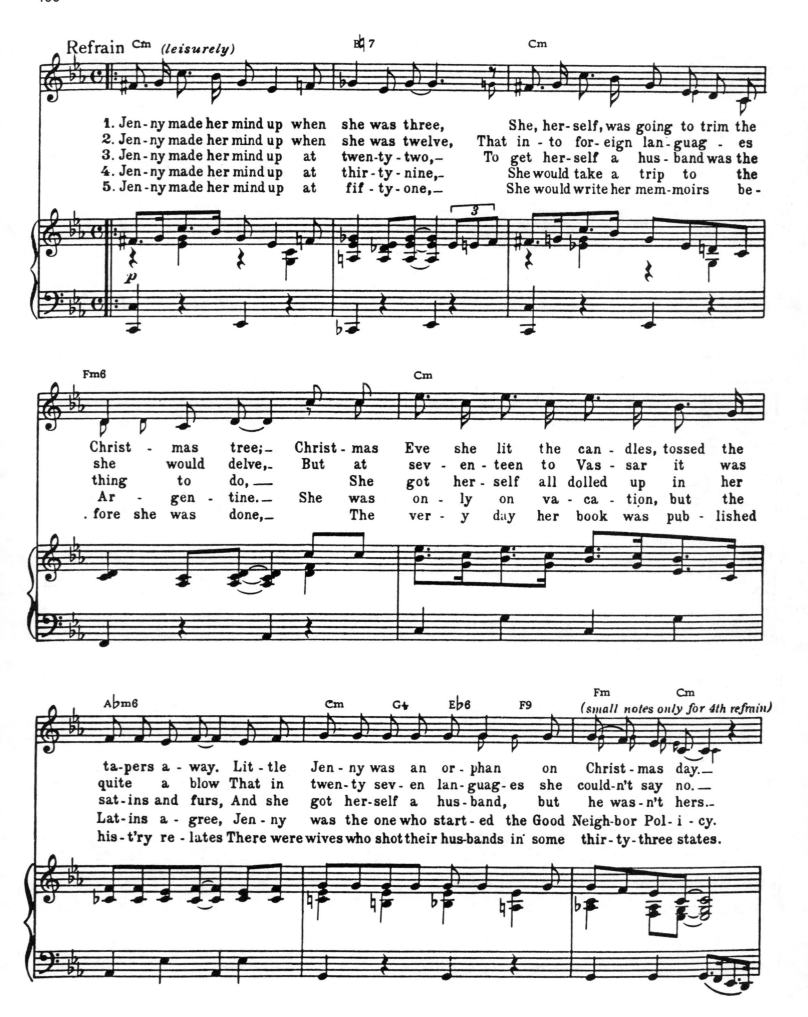

Refrain Cm *(leisurely)*   B♭7   Cm

1. Jen-ny made her mind up when she was three,   She, her-self, was going to trim the
2. Jen-ny made her mind up when she was twelve,   That in-to for-eign lan-guag-es
3. Jen-ny made her mind up at twen-ty-two,—   To get her-self a hus-band was the
4. Jen-ny made her mind up at thir-ty-nine,—   She would take a trip to the
5. Jen-ny made her mind up at fif-ty-one,—   She would write her mem-moirs be-

Fm6   Cm

Christ-mas tree;— Christ-mas Eve she lit the can-dles, tossed the
she would delve,— But at sev-en-teen to Vas-sar it was
thing to do,— She got her-self all dolled up in her
Ar-gen-tine.— She was on-ly on va-ca-tion, but the
-fore she was done,— The ver-y day her book was pub-lished

A♭m6   Cm G+ E♭6 F9   Fm Cm *(small notes only for 4th refrain)*

ta-pers a-way. Lit-tle Jen-ny was an or-phan on Christ-mas day.—
quite a blow That in twen-ty sev-en lan-guag-es she could-n't say no.—
sat-ins and furs, And she got her-self a hus-band, but he was-n't hers.—
Lat-ins a-gree, Jen-ny was the one who start-ed the Good Neigh-bor Pol-i-cy.
his-t'ry re-lates There were wives who shot their hus-bands in some thir-ty-three states.

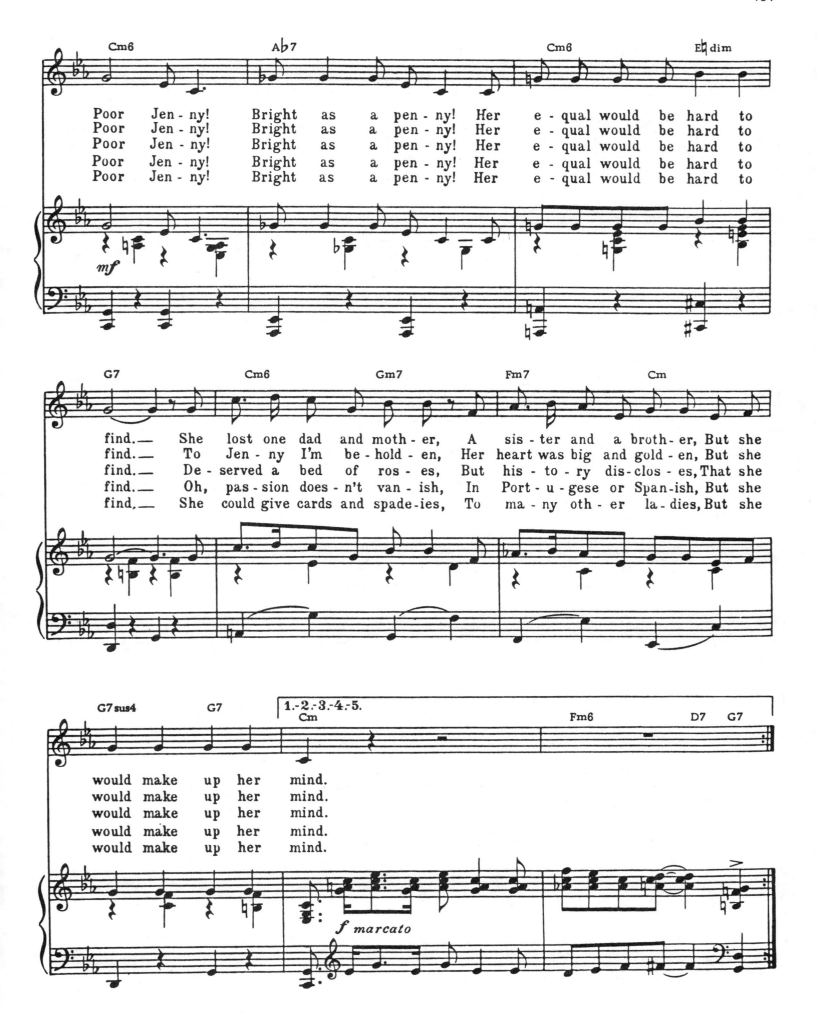

6. Jen - ny made her mind up at sev - en - ty - five,—

She would live to be the old - est wom - an a - live,— But

gin and rum and des - ti - ny play fun - ny tricks— And poor

Jen - ny kicked the buck - et at sev - en - ty - six.—

MY SHIP

My ship has sails that are made of silk,
  The decks are trimmed with gold;
    And of jam and spice
      There's a paradise
        In the hold.

My ship's aglow with a million pearls,
  And rubies fill each bin;
    The sun sits high
    In a sapphire sky
When my ship comes in.

    I can wait the years
    Till it appears—
    One fine day one spring.
    But the pearls and such,
    They won't mean much
    If there's missing just one thing:

I do not care if that day arrives—
  That dream need never be—
    If the ship I sing
    Doesn't also bring
My own true love to me—
    If the ship I sing
    Doesn't also bring
My own true love to me.

MY SHIP

Lyrics by
IRA GERSHWIN

Music by
KURT WEILL

LONG AGO (AND FAR AWAY)

Dreary days are over,
Life's a four leaf clover.
Sessions of depressions are through:
Ev'ry hope I longed for long ago comes true.

Burthen

Long ago and far away
I dreamed a dream one day—
And now that dream is here beside me.
Long the skies were overcast,
But now the clouds have passed:
You're here at last!
Chills run up and down my spine,
Aladdin's lamp is mine:
The dream I dreamed was not denied me.
Just one look and then I knew
That all I longed for long ago was you.

LONG AGO (AND FAR AWAY)

Words by
IRA GERSHWIN

Music by
JEROME KERN

THE MAN THAT GOT AWAY

The night is bitter,
The stars have lost their glitter;
The winds grow colder
And suddenly you're older—
And all because of the man that got away.

No more his eager call,
The writing's on the wall;
The dreams you've dreamed have all
     Gone astray.

The man that won you
Has run off and undone you.
That great beginning
Has seen the final inning.
Don't know what happened. It's all a crazy game.

No more that all-time thrill,
For you've been through the mill—
And never a new love will
     Be the same.

Good riddance, good bye!
   Ev'ry trick of his you're on to.
But, fools will be fools—
   And where's he gone to?

The road gets rougher,
It's lonelier and tougher.
With hope you burn up—
Tomorrow he may turn up.
There's just no let-up the live-long night and day.

Ever since this world began
There is nothing sadder than
   A one man woman looking for
   The man that got away. . .
   The man that got away.

The Gal That Got Away (Concluding Lines)

Ever since this world began
There is nothing sadder than
   A lost, lost loser looking for
   The gal that got away. . .
   The gal that got away.

THE MAN THAT GOT AWAY

Words by
IRA GERSHWIN

Music by
HAROLD ARLEN

Slowly, with a steady insistence

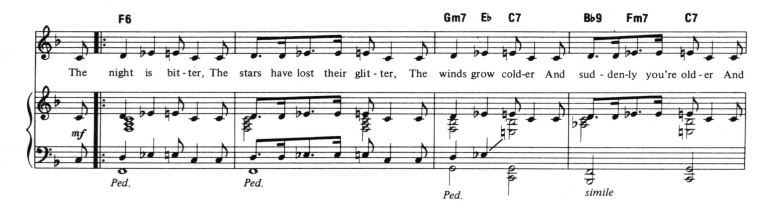

The night is bit-ter, The stars have lost their glit-ter, The winds grow cold-er And sud-den-ly you're old-er And

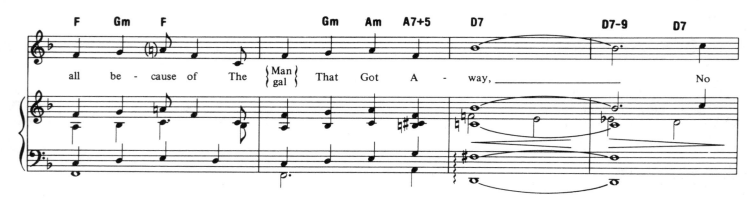

all be-cause of The {Man/gal} That Got A-way, _____ No

more {his/her} eag-er call; _____ The writ-ing's on _ the wall, _____ The

SHOW & MOTION PICTURE INDEX

Song	Composer	Show
Bidin' My Time	George Gershwin	Girl Crazy
Blah, Blah, Blah	George Gershwin	Delicious
But Not For Me	George Gershwin	Girl Crazy
Cheerful Little Earful	Harry Warren	Sweet And Low
Clap Yo' Hands	George Gershwin	Oh, Kay!
Do, Do, Do	George Gershwin	Oh, Kay!
Embraceable You	George Gershwin	Girl Crazy
Fascinating Rhythm	George Gershwin	Lady, Be Good!
A Foggy Day	George Gershwin	A Damsel In Distress
How Long Has This Been Going On?	George Gershwin	Funny Face (Dropped) Rosalie
I Can't Get Started	Vernon Duke	Ziegfeld Follies (1936)
I Got Plenty Of Nuthin'	George Gershwin	Porgy and Bess
I Got Rhythm	George Gershwin	Girl Crazy
I'll Build A Stairway To Paradise	George Gershwin	George White's Scandals (1922)
I've Got A Crush On You	George Gershwin	Strike Up The Band Treasure Girl
Let's Call The Whole Thing Off	George Gershwin	Shall We Dance
Long Ago (And Far Away)	Jerome Kern	Cover Girl
Love Is Here To Stay	George Gershwin	The Goldwyn Follies
Love Is Sweeping The Country	George Gershwin	Of Thee I Sing
Love Walked In	George Gershwin	The Goldwyn Follies
The Man I Love	George Gershwin	Lady, Be Good (Dropped)
The Man That Got Away	Harold Arlen	A Star Is Born (1954)
Mine	George Gershwin	Let 'Em Eat Cake
My Ship	Kurt Weill	Lady In The Dark
Of Thee I Sing (Baby)	George Gershwin	Of Thee I Sing
Oh, Lady Be Good!	George Gershwin	Lady, Be Good!
Oh Me! Oh My!	Vincent Youmans	Two Little Girls In Blue
The Saga Of Jenny	Kurt Weill	Lady In The Dark
Someone To Watch Over Me	George Gershwin	Oh, Kay!
Soon	George Gershwin	Strike Up The Band
Strike Up The Band	George Gershwin	Strike Up The Band
Sunny Disposish	Philip Charig	Americana
Sweet So-And-So	Joseph Meyer, Philip Charig	Sweet And Low
'S Wonderful	George Gershwin	Funny Face
That Certain Feeling	George Gershwin	Tip-Toes
They All Laughed	George Gershwin	Shall We Dance
They Can't Take That Away From Me	George Gershwin	Shall We Dance
Who Cares? (So Long As You Care For Me)	George Gershwin	Of Thee I Sing

IRELAND

DISCOVER ITS BEAUTY

CARSTEN KRIEGER

THE O'BRIEN PRESS
DUBLIN

CARSTEN KRIEGER is a professional photographer based in the west of Ireland. His unique images are highly acclaimed and over the past decade he has become one of Ireland's foremost photographers covering various topics from landscape and nature to architecture and food photography.

He has published numerous books on Ireland's landscape, wildlife and heritage including the popular *Ireland's Wild Atlantic Way* and regularly works for Fáilte Ireland, The UNESCO Burren and Cliffs of Moher Geopark and other clients.

www.carstenkrieger.com

www.irelandsnaturestories.com

First published 2020 by

The O'Brien Press Ltd,

12 Terenure Road East, Rathgar,

Dublin 6, D06 HD27 Ireland.

Tel: +353 1 4923333; Fax: +353 1 4922777

E-mail: books@obrien.ie

Website: www.obrien.ie

The O'Brien Press is a member of Publishing Ireland

ISBN: 978-1-78849-097-9

Text & photographs © copyright Carsten Krieger 2020

Copyright for typesetting, layout, editing, design

© The O'Brien Press Ltd

Designed by Emma Byrne

Maps by Bex Sheridan

7 6 5 4 3 2 1

23 22 21 20

Printed and bound in Poland by Białostockie Zakłady Graficzne S.A.

The paper in this book is produced using pulp from managed forests.

Published in:

DUBLIN
UNESCO
City of Literature

CONTENTS

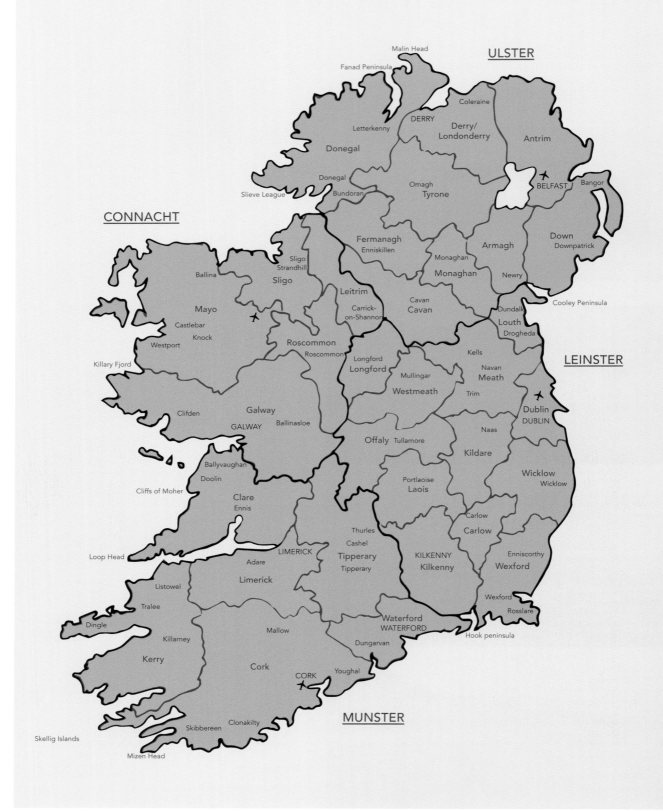

ULSTER

CONNACHT

LEINSTER

MUNSTER

Malin Head

Fanad Peninsula

Coleraine

DERRY

Derry/
Londonderry

Antrim

Letterkenny

Donegal

Donegal

Slieve League

Bundoran

Omagh

Tyrone

BELFAST

Bangor

Sligo
Strandhill

Ballina

Sligo

Fermanagh

Enniskillen

Armagh

Down

Downpatrick

Leitrim

Monaghan

Mayo

Carrick-
on-Shannon

Monaghan

Newry

Castlebar

Cavan

Dundalk

Cooley Peninsula

Knock

Cavan

Louth

Westport

Roscommon

Drogheda

Killary Fjord

Roscommon

Longford

Kells

Clifden

Longford

Mullingar

Navan

Meath

Ballyvaughan

Galway

Westmeath

Trim

Dublin

Doolin

GALWAY

Ballinasloe

DUBLIN

Cliffs of Moher

Offaly

Tullamore

Naas

Clare

Ennis

Portlaoise

Kildare

Wicklow

Laois

Wicklow

Loop Head

Thurles

Carlow

Listowel

LIMERICK

Cashel

Carlow

Enniscorthy

Tralee

Adare

Tipperary

KILKENNY

Wexford

Dingle

Limerick

Tipperary

Kilkenny

Killarney

Mallow

Waterford

Wexford

Kerry

Dungarvan

WATERFORD

Rosslare

Hook peninsula

Cork

Youghal

Skellig Islands

CORK

Skibbereen

Clonakilty

Mizen Head

IRELAND
– A PERSONAL INTRODUCTION

Dusk in the narrow streets of Dingle Town. A fine drizzle is falling from the dark sky and the damp is crawling into clothes and buildings. The sweet smell of turf fires is hanging in the air and gulls are crying in the distance. This was some thirty years ago and is one of my earliest memories of Ireland. In this moment I felt like I had come home.

Since then Ireland has changed considerably. The small island has gone from an underdeveloped country, steeped in tradition and built on tight knit communities, to a modern state with a motorway network, broadband internet, central heating, skinny lattes and hectic lives. Ireland has become richer in a material sense, more cosmopolitan and lives are more comfortable. But the country also has lost something. The old ways, the art of a slow and simple life, are disappearing.

Like many other blow-ins I settled in Ireland because life was different here, unrushed, more

A boreen, or small country road, in the west of Ireland

Top: A rainbow over the Dingle Peninsula
Above left: Beach fun in Kilkee, County Clare
Right: Traditional music session
Opposite left: A statue of Willie Clancy, one of Ireland's most famous traditional musicians, in Milltown Malbay, County Clare
Opposite right: A traditional Irish hearth

focused on things that really matter. There was that slightly rebellious mindset of the Irish, especially when it comes to authorities, that appealed to me. I also came for the landscape, the cliffs and beaches, the mountains and lakes and the wide Irish sky. This much-loved Irish landscape has been shaped over millennia and is intrinsically intertwined with the history of its people. The first settlers built massive tombs and started clearing the vast forests, the arrival of Christianity brought monasteries and cathedrals and the middle ages saw the rise of castles and tower houses. The landscape of Ireland is manmade and in turn the land has shaped men and you will meet a piece of history wherever you go.

It is this landscape that keeps me here. It's the damp and dark winter days, the storms battering the coast and the low clouds that cover the land. It is also the moments the old ways shimmer through, when you chat with a stranger about the weather, when the neighbours bring over an apple pie and when the peat aroma fills the air on a cold winter morning.

This book is not only a visual journey around Ireland, it is also a personal look back on the past few decades travelling around the country. Capturing Ireland with a camera has not always been easy, the infamous Irish weather made sure of that. However it was also this weather that created some of the most memorable moments. Leftover rainclouds hanging around mountaintops, storm force winds pushing the ocean against sheer cliffs, a red sunset after a rainy day, a rainbow just before another heavy shower, a beach covered in hail stones. All this would not be possible without the changeable Atlantic climate that brings low pressure systems to Ireland on a regular basis. It's these systems that bring the light, the colour and the drama the Irish landscape is so famous for. Some of the images in this book date back almost two decades, others have been made especially for this volume. While camera technology has been changed significantly over the years, my approach to photography has not. For me being outside and simply experiencing the landscape is as enjoyable as the photographic process itself. Being hasty never leads to a good image, watching and waiting is a big part of an outdoor photographer's life and being in the right place at the right time is rarely a coincidence.

I hope you will enjoy this book as much as I have enjoyed the past twenty years of travelling, photographing and writing.

Carsten Krieger – June 2020

Left: Traditional butter churning, The Burren, County Clare
Bottom: Traditional ploughing demonstration in the Burren, County Clare
Opposite bottom left: Scones are still being home made in many places.
Opposite bottom right: Fresh vegetables at a traditional farmer's market

A JOURNEY THROUGH HISTORY

When you say 'Ireland', the images that spring to mind are probably things like traditional music, storytelling and poetry, green fields, Guinness and, of course, a long and ancient history. Even the Irish name for this small island at the north-western edge of Europe, surrounded by the Irish Sea and St George's Channel to the east and south and the Atlantic Ocean to the west, dates back to Celtic times; Ireland, or Éire, is believed to take its name from Ériú, the Celtic goddess of the land.

The west coast, especially the mountainous areas of County Kerry and County Galway, get most of the rain that leads to those green Irish fields, and it falls in many shapes and forms. There is the infamous drizzle, a fine, fog-like rain that you hardly notice, but that can drench you within minutes. There also is the soft, warm summer rain falling gently — almost enjoyable. Then there is just rain, dull and grey. And then there is the windswept downpour. This rain comes down almost horizontally in sheets rather than droplets and can last from a few minutes to many hours.

The other fixed component of the Irish weather is the wind. There's rarely a day without a breeze and the voice of the wind is a constant companion. Gales and storms find their way to Ireland on a

Above: Hikers in the Burren

regular basis, often causing death and destruction. One of the worst storms to hit Ireland, known as 'Night of the Big Wind' was on 6 January 1839. Winds were raging at speeds of up to 200 kmh destroying a quarter of all houses in Dublin alone, sinking forty-two ships along the Irish coast and killing an estimated three hundred people. The latest big event happened in 2014 when a series of storms destroyed houses, roads and harbours along the western seaboard. Whole stretches of coast were rearranged during that time. In some places sandy beaches completely disappeared, in other places rocky shores were suddenly covered in sand. Boulder fields were moved several hundred metres inland and cliffs were shattered.

Looking back in time, however, events like these are not out of the ordinary. Ireland has been shaped by the forces of wind and water for millennia, ever since it took up residence in the North Atlantic.

About 55 million years ago the Atlantic Ocean started to form, pushing the American and European continents apart in the process. Part of this process were massive volcanic eruptions that left their marks on the northern parts of Ireland. The basalt rocks that cover parts of County Antrim are reminders of this period.

During the ice ages that started around 17 million years ago, the ice caps of the Arctic and Antarctic extended and retreated in more or less regular cycles. During this time Ireland and parts of northern Europe disappeared again and again under vast ice sheets. These glaciers were the force that shaped the Irish landscape into what we see today. The latest glaciation ended about 10,000 years ago. The tundra-like landscape that became established soon after the glaciers retreated was soon replaced by extensive forests. Birch and hazel were joined by pine first and sometime later by oak and elm. Around 8,000 years ago Ireland was covered in dense forests and some texts claim that it was possible to travel from one end of the island to the other without ever having to touch the ground. This started to change around 5,000 years ago after men arrived in Ireland. The first arrivals were hunter-gatherers who stayed near the coast and had little impact on the Irish landscape. But when the first farmers arrived forest had to make way for farmland and wood was needed as building material.

The last big event in Ireland's natural history happened around 3,000 years ago; the climate changed, it became milder and wetter, conditions that triggered the spread of the blanket bogs of the west and the raised bogs of the midlands. There are numerous signs in the landscape that this change must have happened quickly. There are places where whole forests seem to have been engulfed by the growing bog, leaving behind tree trunks embedded in peat. In northern County Mayo lie the remnants of an old field system, remains of stone walls and buildings that point to a once-thriving farming community. The Céide Fields were discovered under several metres of blanket bog and it is theorised that the farming community, who might have been living here from as early as the stone age, were forced to leave their home when the changing climate made farming impossible in this area. The combination of this new climate and ever more farming activity marked the beginning of the end for the Irish forests. Over the following centuries the forests disappeared and the typical Irish landscape we know today, with its fields and hedgerows, took shape. Only a few pockets of the ancient woodlands survive in spots like Killarney National Park or Glengarriff Nature Reserve.

Ireland's early history in the era before the written word lasted from the arrival of the first hunter-gatherers some 6,000 years ago, through the Bronze Age (from 2500 BC) and into the Iron Age that was marked by the arrival of the Celts (around 600 BC). It was a time of legendary tribes like the Tuatha Dé Danann and the Fir Bolg, warrior groups like the Fianna and mighty heroes like Cú Chulainn and Fionn Mac Cumhaill, and it's difficult to separate fact from fiction. People mainly lived together in family groups of various sizes led by a local chieftains who controlled a certain area of land they needed to raise their livestock and crops. Ringforts, raths and promontory forts date from this

Below left: An Irish cottage
Below right: Horses in the sea

era and were the typical habitation of the time. However, the appearance of High Kings throughout the Irish mythological cycles and the existence of large monuments like the Hill of Tara and the Brú Na Bóinne Complex (including Newgrange and Knowth) make it seem likely that there was a higher hierarchic structure in place at least in some parts of the island.

The documented history in Ireland begins with the arrival of Christianity in the 5th century. The first Christian missionaries arrived from Roman-occupied France and a little bit later from Britain. The best known of those missionaries is, of course, St Patrick, Ireland's patron saint. According to legend Patrick was abducted from his native Britain and sold into slavery in Ireland. It was here, somewhere in Co. Armagh, that he received his calling from God. After fleeing back to his homeland he became a priest in order to return to spread Christianity in the land where he had been held captive for so many years. How much of this is true nobody knows, but it is known that Patrick was only one among many missionaries that travelled to this country.

With Christianity came the Latin language, literature and learning. It was the beginning of what is known as the Golden Age. Monasteries sprang up all over Ireland and soon attracted pilgrims and students from across Europe. Trade increased and towns and cities grew around the monasteries, which soon were not only the centre of religion and learning, but also of power. With trade and power came wealth and this wealth created some beautiful artwork: intricate high crosses, fine metalwork and delicate scriptures. One of the masterpieces of the time is undoubtedly the Book of Kells, which

Below: Surfing lesson in Fanore, County Clare

survives to this day and is on display at Trinity College, Dublin.

The wealth of the Irish monasteries also attracted some unwanted attention. Scandinavian warriors equipped with the most advanced ships of the time made their way to Ireland and in 795 launched their first of many attacks. In the beginning the Vikings used their home bases far north to launch these attacks and concentrated their efforts mainly at the Irish coast. A few decades into their campaign, however, they started to move further inland, using Ireland's rivers, and in 840 they overwintered in Ireland at Lough Neagh and soon after established a first permanent 'longphort', which translates roughly into 'ship-camp', at Ireland's east coast at a place that is known today as Dublin. Over the following decades the Vikings established more permanent bases in Ireland. Many of them grew into thriving cities like Wexford, Waterford, Cork and Limerick. The Vikings also got more involved in local politics and established their own little kingdoms, allied with Irish kings, or went to war to defend their settlements. The Vikings who initially only came for the plunder had become part of Irish society.

Over most of its history medieval Ireland was divided into small kingdoms that fought among themselves. From time to time one leader managed to unite Ireland under his rule as high king. Brian Boru was the first to do so, followed, with interruptions, by a few others, but the Irish were never able to establish a rule of succession and the country stayed divided, which eventually led to the events of 1170 and centuries of oppression.

Diarmuid MacMurrough, king of Leinster with an appetite for high kingship, sought help from the Norman King Henry II of England and Normandy. King Henry II sent one of his nobles, Richard de Clare, also known as Strongbow, and together they captured Waterford and Dublin and started to invade other parts of Ireland. Strongbow married Diarmuid's daughter and succeeded to the throne of Leinster.

At this point Henry II intervened to prevent Strongbow building his own independent kingdom. Henry II invaded Ireland with large forces and soon he had not only secured Strongbow's subjugation, but also that of several other Irish kings. The Normans had – almost overnight – taken over much of Ireland and by 1300 had established castles and power in most parts of the country.

What followed were centuries of plantations, invasions, rebellions, suppression of the Irish culture and way of life. The darkest episode of this time was an event that would change the land and its people forever. What became known as the Great Famine started in 1845. The majority of the Irish population, especially in rural areas, lived on a potato-based diet. Though Ireland produced other crops, as well as meat, those products were mostly exported to England or further abroad. Catastrophe struck when the potato harvest failed for a number of years in a row. A fungal disease known as potato blight destroyed up to 75 per cent of each year's harvest and an inappropriate reaction of the English ruling class caused mass starvation, disease and emigration. After the five years of the Great Famine one million people had died and another million emigrated, a loss of over 20 per cent of the entire population.

The aftermath of the Great Famine saw a new rise of Irish nationalism. Over the centuries of English occupation there had been a number of rebellions, but those had been mainly military and were in the end all overthrown. This new national consciousness produced organisations like the United Irishmen, the GAA, the Gaelic League and Sinn Féin that sought to revive Irish traditions and a political path to independence. Unfortunately the separation from England didn't happen without bloodshed.

The Easter Rising of 1916 lasted only a few days and stayed limited to the centre of Dublin. The Rising and the English response, however, pushed the Irish nationalist movement onwards and led

Left: Rock climbing on the Burren coast
Opposite right: Connemara sheep

to the first Dáil Eireann, an independent government of Ireland, being declared in 1919. Soon after, The War of Independence saw violent incidents and many deaths on both sides. The conflict ended officially in 1921 when a treaty was signed that separated Ireland into Northern Ireland as part of the United Kingdom and the new Irish Free State. For many Republicans, however, this treaty didn't go far enough and the disagreements between the more moderate and the extreme Republicans erupted into civil war in 1921 that lasted for several years and caused the death of a number of leading political figures.

The following decades saw a struggling Irish Free State struggle with severe economic problems, high unemployment and rising emigration. And with renewed unrest in Northern Ireland that grew into a full blown civil war that became known as The Troubles. This new conflict began in the late 1960s and ended only with the signing of the Good Friday Agreement in 1998 that introduced power sharing for a self-governing Northern Ireland.

Since then a peaceful Ireland has prospered and become one of the world's foremost holiday destinations for visitors from home and abroad. Places like the Cliffs of Moher, Killarney and the Ring of Kerry or Connemara have become household names. Irish traditional music and dance have gained an international reputation and are played and practised in countries all over the world. Even Irish food has made a name for itself. If you believe a survey, the Irish Breakfast is one of the main reasons people come to Ireland. The main components of this morning feast are egg, sausages, rashers (thin slices of bacon), black and white pudding and a fried tomato. Sometimes baked beans, mushrooms and potato bread (known as boxty) are thrown in the mix and the whole meal is served with tea or coffee, toast and brown bread. The latter is another Irish specialty and has been around for a long time. This type of bread, also known as soda bread, is made without yeast and uses bicarbonate and buttermilk as a raising agent. The big advantage is that it can be made very quickly, which means a fresh loaf can be ready every morning in time for breakfast. Another famous Irish quick bake is the scone, a sweet roll that is usually served with butter (or cream) and jam. Other typical Irish dishes include the Irish stew (made with lamb and potatoes), bacon and cabbage, and apple pie. Over the past decades Ireland has also made itself a name for its excellent beef, fish and shellfish.

Guinness is another very Irish product that can be found around the globe. Guinness is a stout, a dark beer; other breweries like Beamish or Murphy's also brew stout. A truly Irish invention is the Irish coffee, a mix of strong coffee, whiskey and brown sugar topped by whipped cream. The creation of this potent cocktail is attributed to Joe Sheridan, who was the chef at the Flying Boat terminal in Foynes in County Limerick in the 1940s. Over the past decades coffee in general has become very popular in Ireland and started to rival the traditional beverage, the cuppa tea. The Irish tea culture started in the 19th century and soon the Irish consumed even more tea than their English neighbours and at one time were the top tea drinkers in the world.

Our trip around Ireland will start in the east, in the province of Leinster home not only to Ireland's capital city, Dublin, but also some of the most fascinating historical monuments. From here we will travel clockwise into the province of Munster, home to Ireland's highest mountains, oldest forests, the famous Cliffs of Moher and the limestone karst of the Burren. Our next stop will be Connacht, once the poorest province of the country that today attracts many visitors to the unique landscapes of Connemara and Achill Island, Ireland's holy mountain, Croagh Patrick, and the town with the highest quality of life in Ireland, Westport. Our final stop will be Ulster. This province is shared between Northern Ireland and the counties of Donegal, Monaghan and Cavan that belong to the Republic of Ireland. The landscape of Ulster is one of the most diverse and beautiful in the country and includes the gentle lakelands of Fermanagh and Cavan, the dramatic Mourne Mountains and the wild coast and Glens of Antrim. Looking at images in a book can however not substitute the experience; to really know Ireland you also have to feel and smell the land and see, so I invite you to come and encounter this emerald isle for yourself.

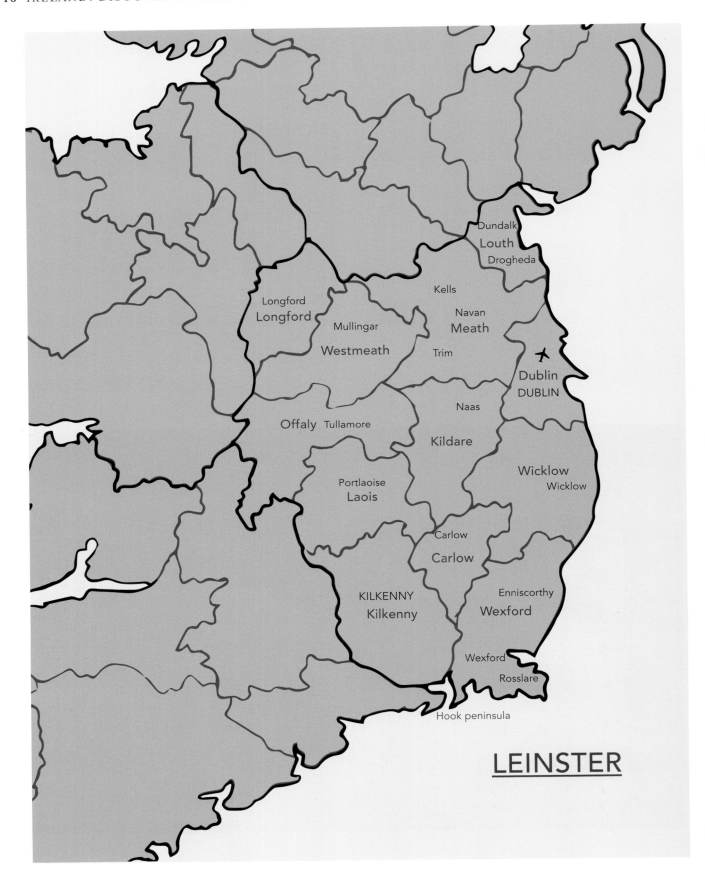

Dundalk
Louth
Drogheda

Kells

Longford
Longford

Navan
Meath

Mullingar
Westmeath

Trim

Dublin
DUBLIN

Offaly   Tullamore

Naas

Kildare

Portlaoise
Laois

Wicklow
Wicklow

Carlow
Carlow

KILKENNY
Kilkenny

Enniscorthy
Wexford

Wexford
Rosslare

Hook peninsula

LEINSTER

LEINSTER

Leinster, made up of twelve counties — Louth, Meath, Westmeath, Longford, Offaly, Kildare, Wicklow, Dublin, Laois, Carlow, Kilkenny and Wexford — is home not only to the capital city, but also to some of Ireland's most fascinating monuments and built heritage.

Top left: Thatcher, County Wexford
Top right: Wexford Wildfowl Reserve
Above: The Cooley Peninsula, County Louth

Top left: Castle Roche, County Louth
Top right: Proleek Portal Tomb, County Louth
Above: An inviting shopping street in Carlingford, County Louth

Top: Dromiskin churchyard, County Louth
Left: Clouds over the countryside, County Louth
Above: Annagassan Harbour, County Louth

Top: Howth Harbour and Ireland's Eye, County Dublin
Above left: The Baily Lighthouse, Howth, County Dublin
Above right: The view from North Bull Island, Clontarf, Dublin

Top: Skerries Strand, County Dublin
Above left: Colliemore Harbour and Dalkey Island, County Dublin
Above right: Vico Baths, County Dublin

Opposite top: The East Pier, Howth Harbour, County Dublin
Opposite bottom: A boat passing Dalkey Island, County Dublin
Top left: Dublin Castle, Dublin
Top right: Georgian Doors, Dublin
Above left: River Poddle, a hidden river under Dublin city centre
Above right: The lights of Dublin city centre reflected in the River Liffey

Dublin is Ireland's capital and largest city. It's thought that a settlement existed here as early as the 7th century AD, but the official recognised foundation date for Dublin is the 10th century. It was established by the Vikings (who arrived in Ireland around 841) and remained under Viking control until the Norman invasion in the 12th century. Under Norman rule Dublin grew into a medieval town and in the 16th century gained importance as the administrative centre of English rule in Ireland. In the following centuries, despite outbreaks of the plague that killed up to half of the inhabitants of the city, Dublin continued to prosper and grow and was for a while in the 18th century the largest city in the British Empire. Most of Dublin's architecture dates from that era when the Wide Streets Commission of the mid-eighteenth century set about a process of demolition and rebuilding to broaden the city's narrow streets. You can see the granite below, brick above facades from this era around the city centre today. Some few prominent Dublin landmarks like Temple Bar and Grafton Street escaped the Georgian reconstruction and kept their medieval character. After some political and economic decline in the 19th and early 20th century Dublin started to prosper again during the Celtic Tiger years and saw considerable new developments.

Today Dublin is not only a thriving capital city, it is also often the first stop for many visitors to Ireland and boasts a number of famous landmarks like Dublin Castle, Trinity College, the Spire, St Stephen's Green, the Ha'Penny Bridge and many others. One of the most visited attractions is the Guinness Storehouse, home of the famous stout that has conquered the world. Arthur Guinness started his brewing business in 1758 and in 1759 signed a 9,000 year lease at the St James's Gate Brewery for 45 pounds per annum. Ten years later he exported his first shipment of Guinness to England and the rest is, as they say, history.

Opposite bottom left: St Stephen's Green, Dublin
Opposite bottom right: The Campanile, Trinity College, Dublin
Above: Ha'Penny Bridge, Dublin, so called because when it first opened there was a toll of a halfpenny to cross it
Bottom left: Gulls on the boardwalk, Dublin city centre
Bottom right: Grafton Street, Dublin

Above: Bray, County Wicklow
Right: View from Bray Head, County Wicklow
Opposite top: Russborough House, County Wicklow
Opposite bottom: Russborough House Library, County Wicklow

Opposite top: Powerscourt Waterfall, County Wicklow
Opposite bottom: The gardens of Powerscourt House, County Wicklow
Above left: Enniskerry, County Wicklow
Above right: Cloghlea, County Wicklow
Below: Lough Tay, County Wicklow

Just south of Ireland's capital lie the Wicklow Mountains, Ireland's largest continuous upland region. This mountain range doesn't rise higher than 925 metres and its appearance is more gentle than dramatic. Rolling hills are covered in blanket bog that looks its best in late summer when the bracken turns golden and the heather blooms purple. At the heart of this ancient landscape — the oldest rocks here are over 500 million years old — lies the Wicklow Mountains National Park, established in 1991. The best-known part of the national park is probably Glendalough, which translates as 'the valley of the two lakes'. As the name suggests this valley, formed by the glaciers that covered the area, hosts two lakes, simply named the Lower Lake and the Upper Lake. At the entrance to the valley sits one of Ireland's most striking historical monuments, the Monastic City of Glendalough. Glendalough was founded in the sixth century by St Kevin and flourished over the following six hundred years into one of the main religious centres in Ireland. Numerous buildings survive to this day including a 30-metre high roundtower, churches, a cathedral and, unique in Ireland, a gateway and remains of an enclosure wall.

Opposite: Winter in the Wicklow Mountains
Above left: Upper Lake, Glendalough, County Wicklow
Above right: The Monastic City, Glendalough, County Wicklow
Below: Mist over the Lower Lake, Glendalough, County Wicklow

Opposite top: Avondale House, County Wicklow
Opposite bottom: Grand Canal, County Kildare
Above left: A reconstructed cell in Wicklow Gaol,
County Wicklow
Above right: Castletown House, County Kildare
Right: St Brigid's Well, County Kildare

Opposite top: Japanese Gardens, The National Stud, County Kildare
Opposite bottom: The National Stud, County Kildare
Top left: Newgrange and the Boyne Valley, County Meath
Top right: Newgrange Entrance, County Meath
Above left: Knowth, County Meath
Above right: Loughcrew Cairn, County Meath

The river Boyne runs for 112km from its source in County Kildare, through County Meath and enters the Irish Sea at Baltray in County Louth. Following the Boyne along its course is a journey through time and history. There is the mythological Hill of Tara, legendary seat of the ancient high kings of Ireland, and Brú na Bóinne (which translates as 'the bank of the Boyne' or 'the bend of the Boyne') with its Neolithic passage tombs. These tombs, Newgrange, Knowth and Dowth, are older than the Egyptian pyramids. Moving forward in time you will find Trim Castle, the biggest Norman fortification in Ireland, and the Hill of Slane with its remains of an early Christian friary that was a centre for learning and religion for centuries. Finally there is the site of the Battle of the Boyne, a clash that was a deciding factor in the fight for the English crown between King James VII and William of Orange in 1690.

Left: St Patrick's Church, Hill of Tara, County Meath
Below: Rag Trees on the Hill of Tara, County Meath
Opposite top: Mound of Hostages, Hill of Tara, County Meath
Opposite bottom: Hill of Slane, County Meath

Opposite top: Old Mellifont Abbey, County Meath
Opposite bottom: Trim Castle, County Meath
Top left: Oldbridge House, County Meath
Top right: Hill of Uisneach, County Westmeath
Above left: Dún na Sí Heritage Park, Moate, County Westmeath
Above right: Lough Derravarragh, County Westmeath

Above left: Jonathan Russell of Nua Canoe, County Westmeath, at work
Above right: Glasson Golf Club, County Westmeath
Below: Sean's Bar, Athlone, County Westmeath
Opposite: St Mel's Cathedral, Longford; it was destroyed in a fire in 2009, but restored to its former glory and reopened in 2014

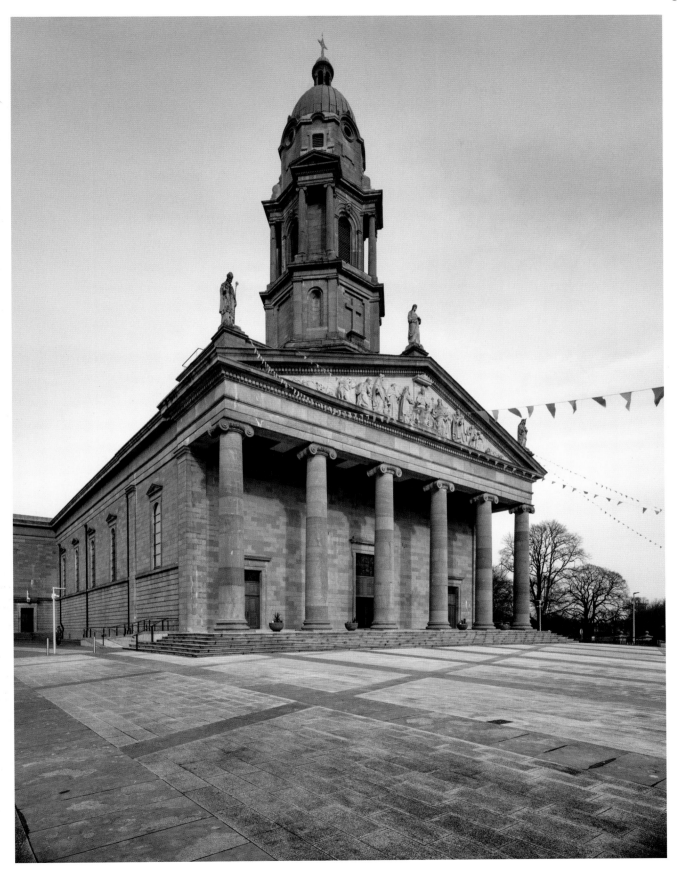

The centre of Ireland is a picture-postcard landscape of fields, hedgerows and rolling hills, dotted with numerous lakes and traversed by rivers and canals. These canals, the Grand Canal and the Royal Canal, were built in the late 18th and early 19th centuries to connect Dublin to Ireland's longest river (and at the time major trading route) the Shannon. Both canals were meant to transport goods as well as passengers between the capital and the midlands. Timing, unfortunately, wasn't good; soon after the introduction of train travel in the late 19th century both canals fell into disuse and disrepair. In the late 20th centuries both canals saw a revival as part of the wider Waterways Ireland scheme. The canals, as well as the long-distance trails that have been established on their banks, have become very popular with pleasure-boaters, cyclists and walkers and are a slightly different way to explore the Irish midlands.

The Grand Canal joins the Shannon at Shannon Harbour, which lies in one of the most interesting areas of the midlands. Only a few kilometres north of Shannon Harbour is one of the biggest towns of the midlands; Athlone sits at the southern end of Lough Ree, one of the three large lakes formed by the Shannon, and started its existence as one of the politically and strategically most important crossings over the Shannon. The ford at Athlone ('Luan's Ford') was not only the only safe crossing for many kilometres, it also marked the border between Leinster and Connacht, the border between the east and the west of Ireland. In the 12th century a bridge was built beside the ford and to protect both ford and bridge a fort was constructed. This fort grew into Athlone Castle, which still stands at the centre of Athlone today. Only a few steps away from the castle lies Seán's Pub which was most likely the very first establishment here, predating both bridge and castle; it is also the oldest pub in Europe.

If you were to get on a boat in Athlone and follow the Shannon south you would soon reach

Left: Belvedere House, County Westmeath
Above: Tullamore Dew Distillery, Tullamore, County Offaly
Below: Early morning mist over the midlands countryside

Clonmacnoise. This monastery was founded in 544 by St Cieran and grew into one of Europe's most important centres for religion, learning and trade. Today the place features the remains of a cathedral, seven churches, two roundtowers and three high crosses. Clonmacnoise was one of the biggest, but still only one of many, early Christian monasteries in the midlands area. Durrow, Rahan, Monaincha and Croghan Hill, to name but a few, were the places where Christianity first took hold in Ireland. Back then the landscape was very different from today. The area was covered in almost impenetrable boglands and those early monasteries became islands in an uninhabitable landscape. Today only a few pockets of those raised bogs, that could reach a depth of more than 10 metres, survive. Most bogs have been drained to be used as pasture and farmland or have been harvested on an industrial scale as fuel for homes and power stations. The largest of those bogs, the Bog of Allen, once covered an area of almost a thousand square kilometres; today only about 10 per cent of the area's raised bog remains intact. Some of those intact boglands can be found in the Lullymore area of County Kildare, which is also home of the Bog of Allen Nature Centre that provides information on the area and Irish boglands in general.

County Kildare, however, is better known for another unique landscape. The Curragh is a vast grassland shrouded in legend and history that has existed in its current state for many centuries. In the past the Curragh has seen meetings of the Fianna, mythical heroes of Irish legend, battles have been fought here and it has been used as a mustering site. The Curragh is most renowned for one thing: horse racing and horse breeding. The history of horse racing on the Curragh goes back to the 18th century. Since then the area has become home to a number of world famous stud farms, including the Irish National Stud, and one of Ireland's best known racecourses, the Curragh Racecourse.

Above left: Seirkieran, County Offaly
Above right: St. Anthony's Well, Killina, County Offaly
Opposite top: Clonmacnoise, County Offaly
Opposite bottom: Lough Boora Parklands, County Offaly

Top left: The Great Telescope at Birr Castle, County Offaly
Top right: Kinnitty Castle Falconry, County Offaly
Above left: National Ploughing Championships
Above right: River Shannon at Banagher, County Offaly

Above: Aghaboe Abbey, County Laois
Bottom left: Ss Peter & Paul Church, Athlone, County Westmeath
Bottom right: Royal Canal at Cloondara, County Longford

Above: Browne's Hill Dolmen, County Carlow
Bottom left: Graiguenamanagh, County Kilkenny
Bottom middle: St Canice's Cathedral, Kilkenny
Bottom right: Kilkenny Castle
Opposite top: Rothe House, Kilkenny
Opposite bottom left: Charleville Castle, County Offaly
Opposite bottom right: Sheep, Kells, County Kilkenny

The counties Wexford, Kilkenny, Carlow and Waterford (the last is actually part of the province of Munster) are often fondly referred to as 'the Sunny South East'. Statistically these counties have the most sunshine hours of the whole of Ireland and luckily the landscape to match. A string of long sandy beaches, interspersed with quaint villages, stretches all the way from Wexford Town at the south-eastern corner of the country to Dungarvan in County Waterford. Along the way the narrow Hook Peninsula interrupts the mostly straight coastline and protrudes into the Celtic Sea. At its tip stands the world's oldest operational lighthouse. Hook Lighthouse probably originated as a simple fire on the low cliffs around the 5th century and was established by the monks of a nearby monastery in Churchtown. The current tower was built in the 12th century and the same monks of Churchtown became the first lighthouse keepers. Hook Lighthouse is not the only historic building on the peninsula. Just up the road from the lighthouse stands Loftus Hall, built in 1350 on the site

Opposite: Dunbrody Famine Ship, New Ross, County Wexford
Above: Hook Lighthouse, County Wexford

of an earlier castle, and known as one of the most haunted houses in Ireland, with stories of demonic
visitors and ghosts. A bit further north you will find Tintern Abbey and Dunbrody Abbey, both dating
from around the 13th century, and Duncannon Fort, a coastal bastion from the 16th century.

Further inland, surrounded by a gentle landscape of fields and winding rivers, lies Kilkenny, one
of Ireland's best preserved medieval cities. Kilkenny originated from a small ecclesiastical settlement
in the 6th century, grew into a monastic centre and subsequently into a city. A number of buildings of
Kilkenny's long history survive to this day: the town walls, the 12th century castle, Shee Alms House,
a Tudor period almshouse, Rothe House, a 16th century townhouse, St Canice's Cathedral and the
Black Abbey, named after the black robes of the Dominican order.

Another impressive monument lies just a few kilometres south of Kilkenny at the outskirts of
the village of Kells. Kells Priory, a 12th century Augustine priory, resembles a fortified castle more
than a place of worship. The inner monastic precinct with church and living quarters and an outer
enclosure, fortified with massive walls and towers.

Above left: Tintern Abbey, County Wexford
Above right: Selskar Abbey, Wexford Town
Below: Wexford Town at sunset

Above: Great Saltee Island, County Wexford
Bottom left: Puffin, Great Saltee, County Wexford
Bottom right: Gannets, Great Saltee, County Wexford

Left: Blackhall Strand,
County Wexford

Ballyvaughan

Doolin

Cliffs of Moher

Clare

Ennis

Thurles

Cashel

Loop Head

LIMERICK

Tipperary

Adare

Tipperary

Limerick

Listowel

Tralee

Waterford
WATERFORD

Dingle

Mallow

Dungarvan

Killarney

Kerry

Cork

Youghal

CORK

Clonakilty

Skibbereen

Skellig Islands

Mizen Head

MUNSTER

MUNSTER

Cork, Kerry and Tipperary are among Ireland's largest counties and they, along with Limerick, Clare and Waterford make up the province of Munster. Kerry is home to Ireland's highest mountain, Carrauntoohil, while Clare boasts the unique karst landscape of the Burren. It's a province rich in natural wonders.

Top: Limerick City
Above left: Copper Coast, County Waterford
Above right: Ardmore, County Waterford

Top: Lismore Castle, County Waterford
Above left: Owenshad River, County Waterford
Above right: Chorister's Hall, Waterford City

Top left: Old and new sit side by side in Waterford City

Top right: The Clock Tower gate on Main Street, Youghal, Co. Cork

Above: Youghal Lighthouse

Left: Rostellan Tomb, County Cork
Top: Kinsale, County Cork
Above: The English Market, which has been serving the people of
Cork City since 1788

Two of Ireland's largest cities can be found in Munster, Cork on the south coast and Limerick in the west. Cork originated as a monastic settlement in the 6th century, but gained importance when the Vikings established a permanent settlement there in the 10th century. The city grew around the River Lee which splits into two channels at the western end of the city and so divides the city centre into islands. At the eastern end of the city the Lee flows into the Celtic Sea. Before reaching the open sea, however, the river has to navigate an intricate island-filled estuary. This naturally sheltered harbour was probably the main reason the Vikings settled here. Apart from Cork City itself there are also harbours at Cobh, Ringaskiddy and Crosshaven making the Lee Estuary and Cork one of the biggest harbour areas in Ireland serving anything from commercial vessels and a fishing fleet to passenger and car ferries and yachts.

Left: Bright buildings in Kinsale, County Cork
Opposite top: Cork Harbour
Opposite bottom: Kanturk Castle, County Cork

Like Cork, Limerick lies at the head of an estuary; just west of the city the River Shannon opens up to form an estuary that stretches on for 100 kilometres. Limerick's city centre is also located on an island, surrounded by the Shannon and the Abbey Rivers. Limerick, too, was founded by Vikings and became one of Ireland's major trading ports. Today commercial shipping has moved away from the city and the big transport vessels use the deep-water port at Foynes a few kilometres west of the city. Both Cork and Limerick are bustling, modern cities that still offer a glimpse into their long history. In Cork you can see Elizabeth Fort, the City Gaol or the English Market to get a glimpse of the city's past. In Limerick there are King John's Castle, the Bishop's Palace and other remains of the medieval city centre.

Opposite: Gougane Barra, County Cork
Below: The Priest's Leap, on the border of County Cork and Kerry

Above left: Old phone box, Timoleague, County Cork
Above right: Michael Collins statue, Clonakilty, County Cork
Opposite top: Baltimore Beacon, County Cork
Opposite bottom: Bantry House, County Cork

Above: Fog on Bantry Bay, County Cork
Below: Uragh Stone Circle, Beara Peninsula, County Cork
Opposite top: Glengarriff and the Caha Mountains, County Cork
Opposite bottom: Garinish Bay, Beara Peninsula, County Cork

Top left: Glanmore Valley, Beara Peninsula, County Kerry

Top right: Castlehaven, County Cork

Bottom: Muckross House, Killarney National Park, County Kerry

Opposite top: Red deer stag, Killarney National Park, County Kerry

Opposite bottom left: Ballaghbeama Gap, Iveragh Peninsula, County Kerry

Opposite bottom right: A statue of King Puck, Killorglin, County Kerry

Above left: Listowel, County Kerry
Above right: The Shop, Knightstown, Valentia Island, County Kerry
Below left: The Clocktower, Knightstown, Valentia Island, County Kerry
Below right: Tetrapod footprints, Valentia Island, County Kerry
Opposite top: Ennis, County Clare
Opposite bottom: Beehive huts on Skellig Michael, County Kerry

Munster's south-western corner is dominated by six peninsulas that stretch out into the Atlantic Ocean. The biggest and most famous is the Iveragh Peninsula, better known as 'the Ring of Kerry'. The interior of this peninsula features Ireland's highest mountain range, the MacGillycuddy's Reeks, with Ireland's highest mountain, the 1038-metre high Carrauntoohil at its centre. To the east of the mountains lies Killarney National Park, Ireland's oldest national park, which was established in 1932. The park covers a landscape of lakes, forests and mountains that seem to have escaped out of a fairytale. Old castles, like Ross Castle at the shores of Lough Leane, and romantic mansions, like Muckross House overlooking the lake of the same name, complete the picture. Killarney National Park is not only picturesque, it's also home to some of the last native oak forests of Ireland and a herd of native red deer. These animals have been roaming the mountains and forests around Killarney for thousands of years and for most of the year are rather elusive. Every year in October, however, they come out into the open for the yearly rut. During these few weeks Killarney's red deer go about their business on the outskirts of Killarney and pretty much ignore any human onlookers. It is one of Ireland's greatest nature events.

While Killarney and the Ring of Kerry are among the most-visited places in Ireland, for many the peninsulas to the south, Beara, and to the north, Dingle, are the more beautiful. The Caha Mountains and the Slieve Miskish Mountains form the backbone of Beara and are made of twisted red sandstone. Deep valleys, some of which are covered in ancient woodland, penetrate into the mountain ranges. Beara's mainly rocky coastline is dotted with small villages and harbours. The colourful Castletownbere is the biggest town on the peninsula and one of the biggest fishing ports in the country.

Opposite: Gallarus Oratory, Dingle Peninsula, County Kerry
Top left: Minard Castle, Dingle Peninsula, County Kerry
Top right: Dingle Town Harbour, Dingle Peninsula, County Kerry
Above: Clogher Head, Dingle Peninsula, County Kerry

Dingle is in many aspects similar to Beara. It also features a mountainous interior and another major fishing harbour. Dingle's coast, however, appears wilder and more rugged, with sheer cliffs and wide sandy beaches. Just off the most westerly tip of the Dingle Peninsula sits a group of six islands, the Blasket Islands. The biggest of them, the Great Blasket, was inhabited until 1953 and gained international fame through a number of books written, originally in Irish but later translated into English, by the islanders. In these books Peig Sayers, Muiris Ó Súilleabháin and Tomás Ó Criomhthain describe their life on the Great Blasket and in doing so give an unique insight into a way of life and traditions that otherwise would have been forgotten. You can visit the Blasket Centre in Dún Chaoin on the Dingle peninsula to learn about the islanders' lives and writing.

Some 30 kilometres south of the Blaskets lie Ireland's most recognisable islands. Skellig Michael (or the Great Skellig) and Little Skellig are not much more than rocky spires rising almost vertically over 200 metres from the Atlantic Ocean. Little Skellig hosts one of the biggest gannet colonies in Ireland. The considerably larger Skellig Michael is home to a number of birds, including the much-loved puffin, but also holds the remains of one of Ireland's most spellbinding historic monuments. Just below the highest point of the islands sits an early Christian monastery consisting of a number of beehive huts, where 6th century monks lived and prayed, a graveyard and a number of stone crosses. Recently Skellig Michael and its monastery featured in the *Star Wars* movies *The Force Awakens* and *The Last Jedi*. Some scenes for the latter movie were also filmed on the Dingle Peninsula and the Loop Head Peninsula, the most northerly of the great peninsulas of Ireland's south west coast.

Loop Head forms the northern boundary of the Shannon Estuary, one of the main shipping lanes into Ireland. There are major ports at Foynes and Limerick, numerous small fishing harbours, power stations at Moneypoint and Tarbert, an aluminium refinery at Aughinish and the airport at Shannon. Despite this industrialisation the Shannon Estuary is also home to a wide variety of wildlife, first and foremost a group of more than a hundred resident bottlenose dolphins. These animals have been living in the estuary for many centuries and have made their appearance as sea monsters in a number of local legends. During the summer dolphin-watch tours are available from Kilrush and Carrigaholt, but it is also possible to observe the animals from the cliffs at Loop Head and other spots along the estuary.

Opposite bottom: Gap of Dunloe, County Kerry
Above left: Louis Mulcahy Pottery, Dingle Peninsula, County Kerry
Above right: Muckross Bindery, Killarney, County Kerry
Below: Conor Pass, Dingle Peninsula, County Kerry

Above: Summer light over Caherconree, Slieve Mish Mountains, County Kerry
Opposite top: The Flying Boat Museum, Foynes, County Limerick
Opposite middle: Shannon dolphins: mother and calf break the surface
Opposite bottom: Moneypoint Power Station, County Clare

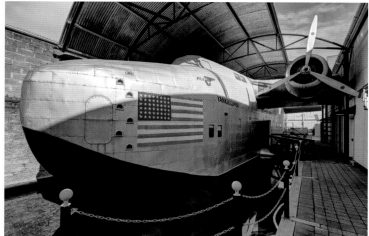

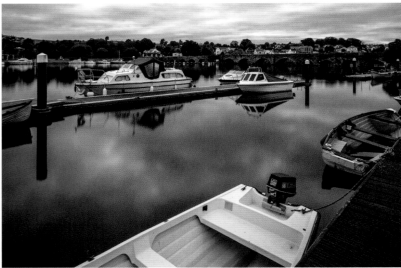

Above: The Lookout, Lough Derg, County Tipperary; Lough Derg has shoreline in three counties, Clare, Galway and Tipperary
Left: Killaloe Harbour, Lough Derg, County Clare
Opposite top: Dromineer Harbour, Lough Derg, County Tipperary
Opposite bottom: Kayakers on Lough Derg, County Tipperary

Above left: Garrykennedy Harbour, Lough Derg, County Tipperary
Above right: Watching the world go by, Doolin, County Clare
Below: Killdysert Harbour, County Clare
Opposite top: Loop Head, County Clare
Opposite bottom: The Bridge of Ross, County Clare

Opposite: Loop Head coastroad, Loop Head Peninsula, County Clare
Above left: Kilkee Promenade, County Clare
Above right: Graveyard overlooking Lahinch beach, County Clare
Below: St Brigid's Well, Moher, County Clare

Top left: Swimmers take part in the Hell of the West Triathlon, Kilkee, County Clare

Top right: Doonbeg, County Clare

Above: Ennistymon, County Clare

Above: Carrigaholt, County Clare
Below left: Foynes Port, County Limerick
Below right: Loop Head Lighthouse, County Clare

The Burren in the north of County Clare is a landscape absolutely distinct from the rest of Ireland; it's a limestone karst landscape, a collection of grey limestone mountains and plateaus with fertile valleys in between. The area is known worldwide for its unusual flora, a mixture of Mediterranean, alpine and arctic plants that grow there. The spring gentian for example, a flower of the high mountains, grows here at sea level. Orchids, lovers of warm, sun-drenched meadows, and mountain avens, flowers of the arctic tundra, can often be found right beside the gentians. The Burren also hosts an unusually rich built heritage. Stone Age monuments like the Poulnabrone Portal Tomb, early Christian buildings, like Templecronan, and medieval tower houses, like Leamenagh Castle, are scattered all over the area.

The Burren and County Clare in general are also renowned for traditional Irish music. The small village of Doolin at the southern borders of the Burren is a mecca for music lovers and the late Willie Clancy from Milltown Malbay or the Kilfenora Céilí Band are household names in Irish folk music.

Below: Mullaghmore, Burren National Park, County Clare
Opposite top left: Bee Orchid, Burren National Park, County Clare
Opposite top right: Irish Saxifrage, The Burren, County Clare
Opposite bottom: Ballyvaughan, County Clare

Opposite top: Limestone pavement, The Burren, County Clare
Opposite bottom left: Cattle winterage, The Burren, County Clare
Opposite bottom right: The Ailwee Caves, The Burren, County Clare
Top: Bishopsquarter, The Burren, County Clare
Left: Music session, Kilfenora, The Burren, County Clare
Above right: Burren Smokehouse, Lisdoonvarna, County Clare

Opposite top: Poulnabrone Portal Tomb, The Burren, County Clare
Opposite bottom: Bunratty Castle, County Clare
Above left: Craggaunowen, County Clare
Above right: Adare, County Limerick
Below: Adare Manor, County Limerick

Above: River Shannon, Limerick City
Left: Thomond Bridge, Limerick City
Opposite top: St Mary's Cathedral, Limerick City
Opposite bottom: The Treaty Stone, Limerick City

The eastern parts of Munster feature gentle landscapes with low mountain ranges and picturesque river valleys. The widest of those valleys is the Golden Vale. It stretches over the counties Limerick, Tipperary and Cork and calls some of the best land for dairy farming in Ireland its own. Overlooking this pastureland is the Rock of Cashel, a striking collection of buildings, including a gothic cathedral and a round tower, sitting on top of a solitary hill. The Rock started its existence as the seat for the kings of Munster, but was donated to the Church in the 12th century and became the seat for the archbishop.

The Rock of Cashel is not the only historic monument in the area. Many of the surrounding market towns have their own piece of history: the impressive castle and the ornamental Swiss Cottage in Cahir, the medieval town walls in Fethard or the Elizabethan manor house, Ormond Castle, in Carrick-on-Suir are just a few examples.

Above: Lough Gur, County Limerick

Above: Glen of Aherlow and Galtee Mountains, County Tipperary
Right: Nenagh Courthouse, County Tipperary

Left: Rock of Cashel, County Tipperary

CONNACHT

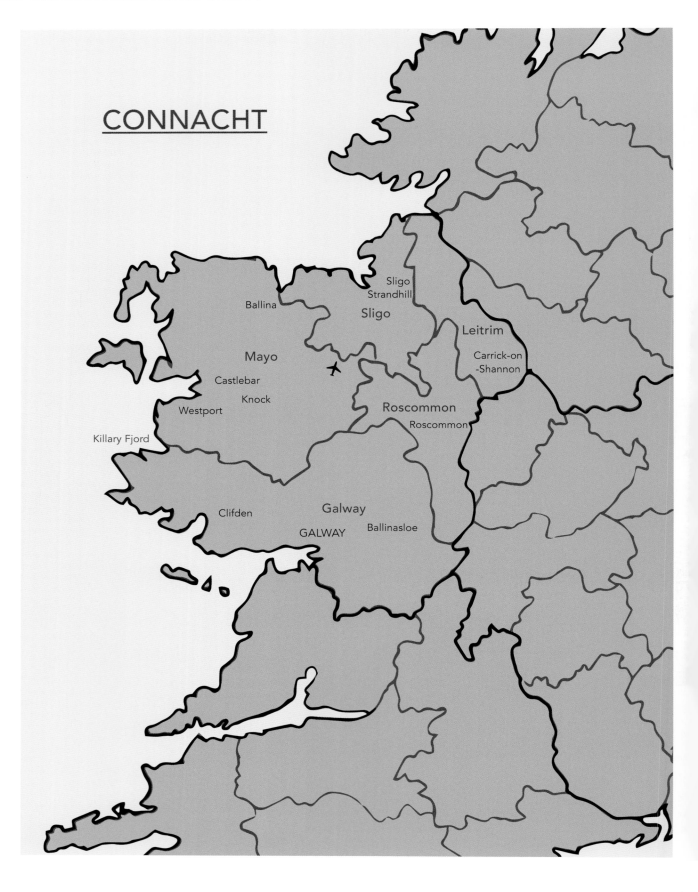

Ballina

Sligo
Strandhill

Sligo

Leitrim

Carrick-on
-Shannon

Mayo

Castlebar

Knock

Westport

Roscommon

Roscommon

Killary Fjord

Clifden

Galway

GALWAY

Ballinasloe

CONNACHT

Connacht, in the wild and beautiful west of Ireland is the smallest of the four provinces, made up of Galway, Leitrim, Mayo, Roscommon and Sligo, but what it lacks in size it makes up for with its rugged coastline, numerous offshore islands and the untamed beauty of Connemara.

Above: Fisherman, Kinvara, County Galway

Opposite top: Kinvara Farmers' Market, County Galway
Opposite bottom: Dunguaire Castle, Kinvara, County Galway
Above: Tyrone House, County Galway
Bottom left: The Claddagh, Galway City
Bottom right: Galway Marina, Galway City

Opposite: Seafront at Salthill, Galway
Above left: Statue of Oscar Wilde and Eduard Vilde, Galway City
Above right: Summer Sunday at the Spanish Arch, Galway City
Right: Visitors to the Galway International Arts Festival

Galway is one of the largest cities on Ireland's west coast. Known as The City of the Tribes, it takes its nickname from the fourteen merchant families, The Tribes of Galway, who ruled there in the middle ages. The city originally grew up around a castle dating back to 1124. In medieval times, Galway was one of the richest cities in Ireland and the principal port for trade with Spain and France. A reminder of this time is the Spanish Arch, part of the old town wall that stands at the mouth of the River Corrib.

On the other side of the river lies what was once the old Claddagh village. Today the area is part of the city, but originally the Claddagh was a small fishing village just outside the city walls. The Claddagh is of course best known for the ring of the same name, shaped in the form of two clasped hands holding a crowned heart. According to legend the ring was created by Richard Joyce, a native of Claddagh, who was kidnapped by pirates and sold into slavery where he learned his craft as a jeweller. After his escape Joyce returned to the Claddagh where he set up his jewellery business and created the first Claddagh Ring.

Opposite bottom: Clonfert Cathedral, County Galway
Above: Dawn at Lough Corrib, County Galway

Above: Lough Corrib, County Mayo; a small part of north east Lough Corrib has its shoreline in County Mayo
Below left: Keith Geoghegan, Connemara sheep farmer and owner of the Glengowla Mines
Below right: A candle for the miners, Glengowla Mines, Connemara, County Galway
Opposite top: Flannery Bridge, Connemara, County Galway
Opposite bottom: Clifden, Connemara, County Galway

Opposite top: Clifden Castle, Connemara, County Galway

Opposite bottom: Gorteen Bay, Roundstone, Connemara, County Galway

Top left: A curious resident at Manor Connemara Ponies, Connemara, County Galway

Top right: Evening light on the Twelve Bens, Connemara, County Galway

Above left: Roundstone harbour, Connemara, County Galway

Below: Turf stacks, Inagh Valley, Connemara, County Galway

Connemara is a wild and intriguing landscape. The interior is dominated by two mountain ranges, the Maumturk Mountains and the Twelve Bens. From the foothills of these mountains stretch vast areas of blanket bog, dotted with numerous lakes. The mainly flat coastline runs in twists and turns, forming long inlets and sheltered bays that hold some of Ireland's most beautiful, sandy beaches. There are also the famous coral beaches of Connemara, which consist of the remains of coralline algae and seashells that have been smoothed by the constant wave action and feel like soft gravel underfoot. One of those inlets that make up Connemara's coast stretches for sixteen kilometres; Killary Harbour marks the northern border of the area and is Ireland's only fjord, formed when glaciers cut a deep valley into the landscape.

Clifden is the largest town in Connemara and often referred to as its capital. It was founded in the early 19th century by John D'Arcy, a member of the powerful D'Arcy family who resided at Clifden Castle, which today stands at the outskirts of the town. It was his ambition to create a town at the western edge of Connemara. After a slow start the population rose from only 290 in 1821 to 1,257 ten years later. In the following years the town prospered further, there was a fishing harbour, a brewery, distillery and a mill and eventually Clifden got its own police station, jail and courthouse.

Right: Gardener's
Cottage, Kylemore Abbey,
County Galway
Below: Kylemore Abbey,
Connemara, County
Galway

Above: Derryclare Lough, Connemara, County Galway
Below: Sunset on Inisheer island, County Galway

Above: Stone walls on Inisheer Island, County Galway
Below left: Farm on Inisheer Island, County Galway
Below right: Killary Harbour, Connemara, County Galway

Opposite top: Croagh Patrick,
County Mayo
Opposite bottom:
Aghagower, County Mayo
Right: Westport, County Mayo
Bottom left: Westport House,
County Mayo
Bottom right: Westport,
County Mayo

According to a number of surveys Westport is the town with the highest quality of life in Ireland and a stroll down its attractive, bustling streets full of all manner of independent shops and cafés would convince you of it. The picturesque town sits at the south-eastern corner of Clew Bay which according to legend has one island for every day of the year. In reality there 117 islands, which are are drumlins, elongated hills, that were formed by retreating glaciers and then partially flooded by the rising sea levels. They are best viewed from the summit of Croagh Patrick that rises at the southern shores of the bay. Croagh Patrick, also known as The Reek, is Ireland's holy mountain named after the patron saint, St Patrick. The legend tells of St Patrick praying and fasting on the summit of Croagh Patrick for forty days during which time he also banished all snakes from the island of Ireland by chasing them into the sea. To remember St Patrick's time on the mountain, a pilgrimage happens each year on the last Sunday of July, Reek Sunday, which still attracts thousands.

The views from the summit are breathtaking — assuming Croagh Patrick isn't covered in clouds. The waters of Clew Bay, surrounded by a green tapestry of fields, lie in the foreground and in the distance the outline of the Nephin Beg range and the seemingly endless blanket bogs of Ballycroy and Bangor Erris are visible in the distance. Parts of this unique bogland are protected in the Ballycroy National Park. One of the main building blocks of bogland habitat is the sphagnum moss that can hold up to twenty times its own weight in water. Sphagnum ranges from a pale grey when dry to a vibrant mix of green, yellow and red tones when damp. In-between the mossy mats thrive a multitude of wildflowers like the carnivorous sundew, the fluffy bog cotton and the vibrant bog asphodel.

Above left: Westport Golf Club, County Mayo
Above right: Slievemore, Achill Island, County Mayo
Left: Pollagh Harbour and Minaun Cliffs, Achill Island, County Mayo

Left: The Deserted Village, Achill Island, County Mayo
Right: Ballycroy National Park, County Mayo
Below: Eagle Island, Mullet Peninsula, County Mayo

Above: Rossport, County Mayo
Left: Collecting seaweed, Ballycroy,
County Mayo

Left: Ballintubber Abbey, County Mayo
Bottom: Lough Mask, County Mayo

Opposite top: The Céide Fields, County Mayo
Opposite bottom: Enniscrone, County Sligo
Above left: Sea kayaking, Enniscrone, County Sligo
Above right: Carrowkeel, County Sligo
Below: Winter dawn at Lough Gill, County Sligo

Above: Parke's Castle, County Leitrim
Opposite top: Spring Forest, Dooney Rock, Lough Gill, County Sligo
Opposite bottom: Drumcliffe Churchyard, County Sligo, burial place of W.B. Yeats

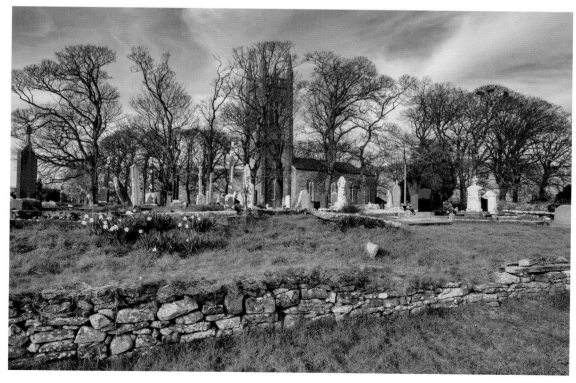

Above: Glencar, County Leitrim
Left: Glencar Waterfall, County Leitrim

Above: Gleniff Horseshoe, County Sligo

Above left: Rosses Point, County Sligo
Above right: Classiebawn Castle, County Sligo

Below: Ben Bulben seen from Back Strand, Grange, County Sligo

Sligo, Leitrim and Roscommon are the northernmost counties of Connacht and present a very different landscape from the barren boglands of north Mayo. The western parts of County Sligo and County Leitrim feature a gentle coastline with sandy beaches, dunes and rocky shores. Only a few kilometres inland rise a number of flat-topped mountains with sheltered valleys in between. One of those mountains is the iconic Ben Bulben that overlooks the small village of Drumcliffe where one of Ireland's greatest poets and recipient of the Nobel Prize for literature lies buried. W.B. Yeats was born in Dublin, but spent much of his childhood in County Sligo and although he rarely returned later in life, the landscape of Sligo left a lasting impact and features in several of his poems. Ben Bulben and Glencar Waterfall appear in 'Towards Break of Day', Rosses Point in 'The Stolen Child' and Lough Gill in 'The Lake Isle of Innisfree'.

The area also features many historic monuments like the cairn of the legendary Queen Maeve. The cairn, the biggest of its kind in Ireland, sits on top of Knocknarea Mountain, a solitary table mountain west of Sligo Town. Just east of the mountain lies the Carrowmore Megalithic Cemetery, a collection of thirty Neolithic portal tombs and stone circles that date back to the 4th millennium BCE.

Opposite: Lough Arrow, County Sligo
Above: Elphin Windmill, County Roscommon
Right: Templeronan, Lough Gara, County Sligo

Above left: Lough Key, County Roscommon
Above right: River Shannon / Lough Allen Canal, Battlebridge, County Leitrim
Below: Lough Allen Canal, County Leitrim.
Opposite: Carrick-On-Shannon, County Leitrim

Right: Lough Ree, Ballyleague,
County Roscommon, Ireland
Below: Roosky, County Leitrim
Opposite top: Portumna
Workhouse, County Galway
Opposite bottom: The Shannon
at Portumna, County Galway

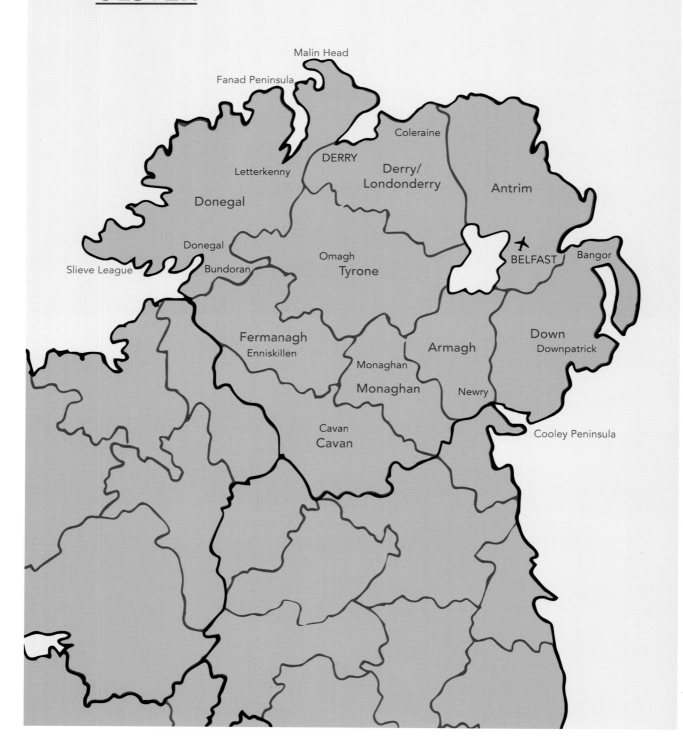

ULSTER

Malin Head

Fanad Peninsula

Coleraine

DERRY

Letterkenny

Derry/
Londonderry

Antrim

Donegal

Donegal

BELFAST

Bangor

Slieve League

Bundoran

Omagh
Tyrone

Fermanagh
Enniskillen

Down
Downpatrick

Monaghan

Armagh

Monaghan

Newry

Cavan
Cavan

Cooley Peninsula

ULSTER

Ulster — which includes the six counties of Northern Ireland — boasts one of the most diverse landscapes in the country and from the gentle lakelands of Fermanagh and Cavan, to the wild coasts and the imposing Mourne mountains.

Top: Surfers, Bundoran, County Donegal
Above: Sunset surfer, Donegal Bay, County Donegal

Left: Bundoran, County Donegal
Right: Murvagh, County Donegal
Bottom: Lough Eske, County Donegal

Opposite top: Killybegs, County Donegal
Opposite bottom: Slieve League, County Donegal
Top: The valley of Glencolmcille, County Donegal
Above left: Standing Stone, Glencolmcille, County Donegal
Above right: Essaranka Waterfall, County Donegal

Above: Lough Derg, County Donegal
Below: Tramore Strand, Portnoo, County Donegal
Opposite top: Crohy Head, County Donegal
Opposite bottom: Errigal Mountain, County Donegal

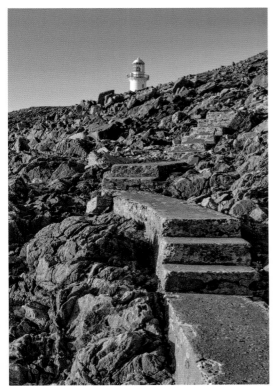

Opposite top left: The Poisoned Glen, County Donegal
Opposite bottom: Glenveagh National Park, County Donegal
Top left: Burtonport, County Donegal
Top right: Aranmore Island, County Donegal
Above left: Lighthouse, Arranmore Island, County Donegal
Above right: Donegal donkey

Donegal, sometimes labelled 'the forgotten county', is different. It is part of the Republic of Ireland, but is only connected to it through a narrow land corridor and shares most of its border with the counties of Northern Ireland. This geographical and economic isolation resulted not only in the lowest density of population in Ireland, it also encouraged Donegal to develop and preserve a very strong local identity, culture and way of life. Donegal's wild landscape reflects this identity. Old, weathered mountain ranges alternate with vast blanket bogs. The coast is a mix of wide, sandy beaches and dramatic cliffs, like at Slieve League, arguably one of the most beautiful and impressive spots in Ireland. Fearless walkers can not only admire the cliffs from a distance, but can walk along the top of the One Man's Path with sheer drops of up to 600 metres on both sides.

Above: Ards Forest Park, County Donegal
Opposite left: Doe Castle, County Donegal
Opposite right: Fanad Lighthouse, County Donegal

Apart from its wonderful landscape (as well as Slieve League, Donegal has Glenveagh National Park, Mount Errigal, the Poisoned Glen, the Inishowen Peninsula, the Rosses, the Fanad Peninsula – all spectacularly beautiful), Donegal is well known for a very special fabric, Donegal tweed. This tweed was and still is made by hand from local materials and transformed into caps, suits and waistcoats.

Music is another well-known Donegal export. Traditional or traditional-influenced artists from Donegal like Clannad, Altan or Enya, as well as rock acts like Rory Gallagher, who was born in Ballyshannon, County Donegal, gained international success.

County Donegal hosts one of the largest *Gaeltacht* (or Irish-speaking) areas in Ireland. Road signs and many shop and pub displays are in Irish only and the vernacular language is also Irish. This is especially evident on the offshore islands, Arranmore, Tory and Inishbofin, where it is very unusual to hear any English.

Top: John Heena at work in Studio Donegal, a woollen mill and weavers on the Wild Atlantic Way
Above left: Ballyliffin Golf Club, County Donegal
Above right: Doagh Famine Village, Inishowen Peninsula, County Donegal

Top left: Buncrana, Inishowen Peninsula, County Donegal
Top right: A farm in the Urris Hills, Inishowen Peninsula, County Donegal
Above: An Gríanán of Aileach, County Donegal

Above: Moville Pier, Inishowen Peninsula, County Donegal
Below: Inishowen Lighthouse, Inishowen Peninsula, County Donegal
Opposite top: Lloyd's Signal Tower, Malin Head, County Donegal
Opposite bottom: A farm at Malin Head, County Donegal, Ireland's most northerly point

Opposite: Mussenden Temple, Downhill, County Derry/Londonderry
Above: City Walls, Derry/Londonderry

Above: The Peace Bridge, Derry/Londonderry
Opposite top and bottom: Bogside murals, Derry/Londonderry

Derry/Londonderry is the second largest city in Northern Ireland and is located in the county of the same name close to the border with County Donegal. Derry's history goes back to the 6th century when St Colmcille founded a monastery here. Derry city is a product of the 17th-century Plantation of Ulster, which aimed to settle Ulster with a population supportive to the English Crown. In 1613 Derry received a royal charter, was renamed 'Londonderry' and was rebuilt from the ground up. Among the first structures to be erected were the massive town walls and gates, which still dominate the city today. Over the following centuries Derry/Londonderry, was often at the centre of the Irish struggle for independence. During the War of Independence (1919-1921) the IRA fought a guerilla war with the British Army in the streets of the city, which sparked further violence between the Catholic and Protestant citizens. After the end of the War of Independence it suddenly became a border city and was cut off from its traditional trading routes with County Donegal, with significant economic consequences. Over the following decades the city kept struggling and tension among its citizens was building. A growing civil rights movement became open riot in 1969 when residents of Derry's bogside clashed with the Royal Ulster Constabulary. What became known as the 'Battle of the Bogside' lasted for three days and is seen as the start of the Troubles in Northern Ireland.

Today the city is known for a rich cultural scene and became the first UK City of Culture in 2013.

Opposite: Mountsandel Wood, Coleraine, County Derry/Londonderry
Above left: Ardboe High Cross, County Tyrone
Above right: Promenade and Arcadia Cafe, Portrush, County Antrim
Right: Ballintoy Church, County Antrim

Opposite top: White Rocks, Portrush, County Antrim
Opposite bottom: Dunluce Castle, County Antrim
Above: Giant's Causeway, County Antrim
Right: Basalt columns, Giant's Causeway, County Antrim

Opposite top: Countryside, County Antrim
Opposite bottom: The Dark Hedges, County Antrim
Above: Dunseverick Castle, County Antrim
Below: Kinbane Castle, County Antrim

Above: Whitepark Bay, County Antrim
Opposite: Elephant Rock, Ballintoy, County Antrim

Opposite top: Ballintoy Harbour, County Antrim
Opposite bottom: Ballycastle Beach, County Antrim
Right: Pan's Rock Bridge, Ballycastle, County Antrim
Below: Ballycastle, County Antrim

County Antrim is one of the most picturesque areas in Ireland. The scenery of Ireland's north-east corner, known as the Antrim Coast and Glens, seems to have escaped from a fantasy movie and in fact a number of locations have been featured in *Game of Thrones*. Antrim's Dark Hedges became Kingsroad, Ballintoy became the Iron Islands and Murlough Bay became Slavers' Bay, to name but a few. Sheer cliffs, wide bays with sandy beaches, small and sheltered harbours, ominous castle ruins and bustling villages make up the Antrim coast. From here nine very different valleys open up into the Antrim Plateau. Picturesque names like Glenarm, 'the Glen of the Army', or Glencorp, 'the Glen of the Slaughtered', give a glimpse of the rich and often bloody history of Antrim's Coast and Glens. The most famous of the glens is Glenariff, often referred to as the 'Queen of the Glens', which was, like the other glens, formed by glaciers that once covered the area. Glenariff is unique among the nine glens and forms a narrow gorge through which the Glenariff and Inver Rivers tumble over dramatic waterfalls. The steep walls of the gorge are covered in mosses and ferns and are overshadowed by tall trees.

The best-known place on Antrim's coast is probably the Giant's Causeway, a natural formation of hexagonal basalt columns that disappear into the Atlantic Ocean only to reappear further north at the coast of Scotland. According to legend this causeway was built by the Irish hero Fionn Mac Cumhaill who was challenged to a fight by the Scottish giant, Benandonner. In one version of the story the rivals meet halfway and Fionn defeats Benandonner, destroying the causeway in the process. In another version Benandonner visits Fionn's house and meets Fionn's wife, and Fionn acting as his own baby son. Benandonner, scared by the size of the 'baby', makes a hasty retreat, dismantling the causeway behind him. Geologists tell us that that the Giant's Causeway was formed by volcanic eruptions that happened around fifty million years ago. These eruptions also formed the Antrim Plateau and many other features along the coast.

At the very southern end of the Causeway Coastal Route, which starts at Derry/Londonderry, lies Northern Ireland's capital, Belfast. This city will always be associated with one of the biggest stories in seafaring history, the *Titanic*. The *Titanic* was built at the shipyard of Harland & Wolff on Queen's Island – today known as the *Titanic* Quarter – between 1909 and 1912. *Titanic* left Belfast for Southampton in April 1912 and from there started her ill-fated journey across the Atlantic.

Opposite: Glenballyemon, County Antrim
Below left: Glenariff, County Antrim
Below right: Glenariff Forest Park, County Antrim

Above: Bluebells at Portglenoe Forest, County Antrim
Below left: A farm in the Antrim countryside
Below right: Bushmills Distillery, County Antrim
Opposite top: Slemish Mountain, County Antrim
Opposite bottom: Winter on the Antrim Plateau, County Antrim

Above: Carnlough, County Antrim
Below left: Whitehead, County Antrim
Below right: Titanic Belfast building, Belfast, County Antrim

Above: View over Belfast, County Antrim
Below left: Belfast Castle, Belfast, County Antrim
Below right: Belfast Zoo, Belfast, County Antrim

Left: Jordanstown, Belfast, County Antrim
Below: Donaghadee Harbour, County Down

Above left: Ballycopeland Windmill, County Down
Above right: Mount Stewart, County Down
Below: Nendrum Monastery, County Down

Above and below: Countryside and Mourne Mountains, County Down
Opposite top: Silent Valley, Mourne Mountains, County Down
Opposite bottom: Harry Avery O'Neill's Castle, Newtownstewart, County Tyrone

Opposite top: Sion Mills Flax Mills,
County Tyrone
Opposite bottom: Ogham Stone,
Sperrin Mountains, County Tyrone
Above: Gortin Glen, Sperrin Mountains,
County Tyrone
Right: Old farm, Sperrin Mountains,
County Tyrone

Opposite top: Summer dawn, County Armagh
Opposite bottom: Killeavy Old Churches, Slieve Gullion, County Armagh
Top left: Ringfort replica, Navan Fort, County Armagh
Top right: Armagh Demesne, County Armagh
Bottom left: St Patrick's Cathedral, Armagh, County Armagh
Bottom right: Armagh City, County Armagh

Left: Loughgall, County Armagh
Bottom: Enagh Lough, County Armagh

Above: Lough Barry,
Inishmore, Upper
Lough Erne, County
Fermanagh
Right: Crom Church,
County Fermanagh

Above: Fisherman, Upper Lough Erne, County Fermanagh
Opposite top: Enniskillen Castle, County Fermanagh
Opposite bottom: Janus Figure, Lower Lough Erne, County Fermanagh

The border counties of Fermanagh (in Northern Ireland) and Cavan (in the Republic of Ireland) share a landscape known as the Irish Lakelands. At the heart of this watery wonderland lies the River Erne. It rises just south of Cavan Town and first flows westward and forms Lough Gowna. After exiting the lake the Erne turns northward. For the following fifty kilometres or so it becomes difficult to distinguish the river as it winds its way through a maze of interconnected lakes nestling among the drumlin hills of County Cavan and County Fermanagh. Lough Oughter almost seamlessly becomes Upper Lough Erne and only after the river reaches the town of Enniskillen does it widen into a proper lake, Lower Lough Erne. This lake, especially its southern part, is dotted with islands, many of which host remains of early Christian settlements.

Only a few kilometres west of the Erne and its lakes rises Ireland's longest river, the Shannon. The first attempt to connect the Erne with the Shannon was made in 1780 with the grand plan to eventually hook up both with Lough Neagh. It took, however, another seventy years until the first boat was able to use the canal that now connected the Upper Lough Erne with Leitrim Village on the Shannon. Commercially the canal never became the success it was anticipated to be and soon fell into disrepair. Only with the increase in pleasure boating on the Shannon in the late 20th century came the idea to resurrect the connection between the Shannon and Erne. After intensive restoration work the Shannon-Erne-Waterway opened in 1994 and is now a tranquil haven for cruisers and barges, as well as anglers, cyclists and walkers along its banks.

Opposite: Drumlane Abbey, County Cavan
Above: Cuilcagh Mountains, County Fermanagh
Right: Marble Arch Caves, County Fermanagh

Opposite: Lough Oughter Castle, County Cavan
Above: Annaghmakerrig Lough, County Cavan
Below: Lough Gowna, County Cavan

Above: Monaghan Town, County Monaghan

Right: The Birdy Tree, a former meeting place for cattle dealers, Carrickmacross, County Monaghan